Carrying the few possessions they could salvage, homeless Japanese families pick their way through the wreckage of Kobe, fire-bombed by American B-29s in May of 1945. In spite of such hardships, the Japanese at this point were preparing all-out resistance to an expected invasion by the Allies.

JAPAN AT WAR

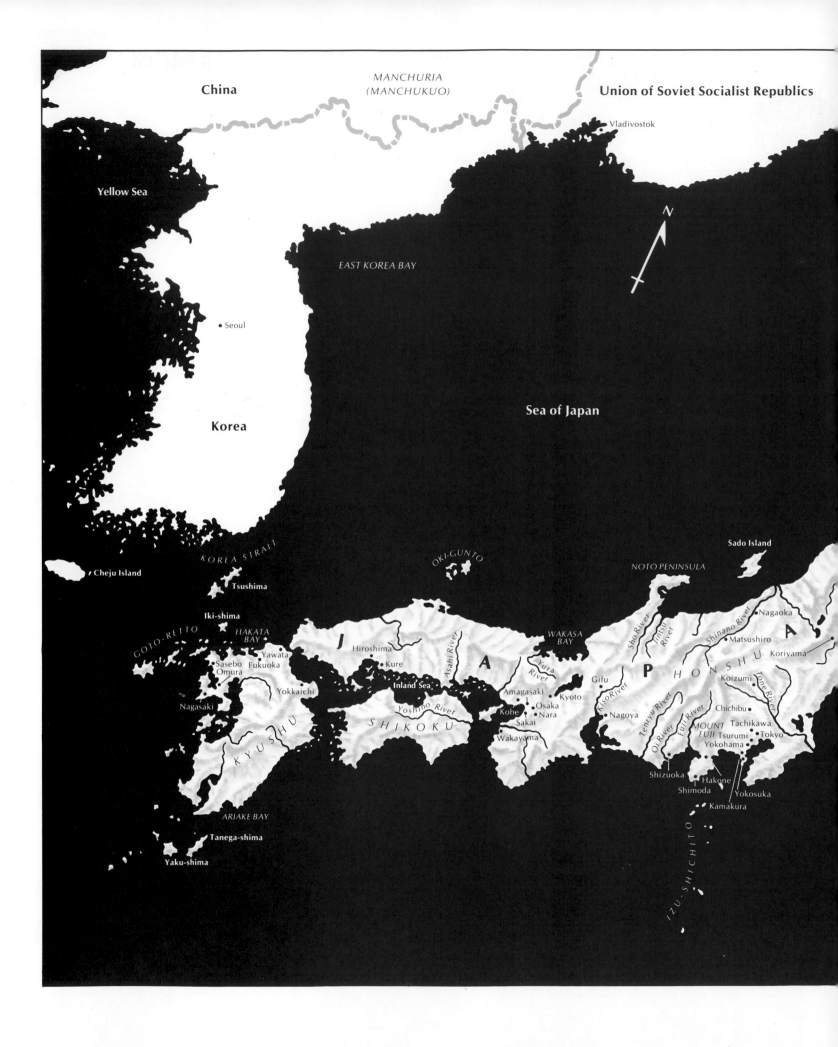

A VULNERABLE ISLAND NATION

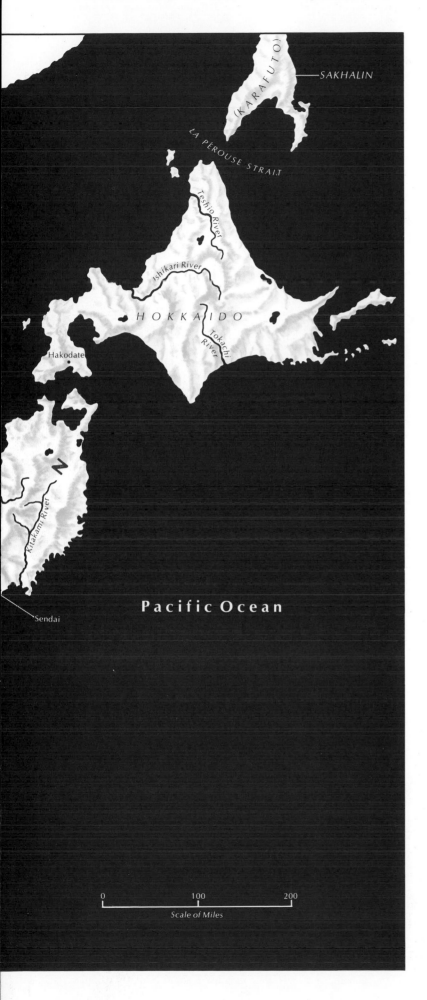

SAKHALIN

(KARAFUTO)

LA PÉROUSE STRAIT

Teshio River

Ishikari River

HOKKAIDO

Tokachi River

Hakodate

Kitakami River

Pacific Ocean

Sendai

0	100	200

Scale of Miles

On the eve of World War II, Japan was the most heavily industrialized nation in Asia, with 40 per cent of its 73 million citizens packed into sprawling manufacturing cities —chiefly Tokyo, Osaka, Nagoya, Kyoto, Kobe and Yokohama. But the island nation's dependence on shipping for essential raw materials made it vulnerable to submarine blockade, and the concentrations of war plants made tempting targets for enemy bombers. Between the mounting shortage of basic necessities and the increasing impact of American strategic-bombing raids, Japanese civilians probably suffered more casualties than their fighting men overseas, and endured as much hunger and hardship as any other people in the War.

WORLD WAR II · TIME-LIFE BOOKS · ALEXANDRIA, VIRGINIA

BY THE EDITORS OF TIME-LIFE BOOKS

JAPAN AT WAR

Time-Life Books Inc.
is a wholly owned subsidiary of
TIME INCORPORATED

Founder: Henry R. Luce 1898-1967

Editor-in-Chief: Henry Anatole Grunwald
President: J. Richard Munro
Chairman of the Board: Ralph P. Davidson
Executive Vice President: Clifford J. Grum
Chairman, Executive Committee: James R. Shepley
Editorial Director: Ralph Graves
Vice Chairman: Arthur Temple

TIME-LIFE BOOKS INC.

Managing Editor: Jerry Korn
Executive Editor: David Maness
Assistant Managing Editors: Dale M. Brown
(planning), George Constable, Thomas H. Flaherty Jr.
(acting), Martin Mann, John Paul Porter
Art Director: Tom Suzuki
Chief of Research: David L. Harrison
Director of Photography: Robert G. Mason
Assistant Art Director: Arnold C. Holeywell
Assistant Chief of Research: Carolyn L. Sackett
Assistant Director of Photography: Dolores A. Littles

Chairman: Joan D. Manley
President: John D. McSweeney
Executive Vice Presidents: Carl G. Jaeger,
John Steven Maxwell, David J. Walsh
Vice Presidents: George Artandi (comptroller);
Stephen L. Bair (legal counsel); Peter G. Barnes;
Nicholas Benton (public relations); John L. Canova;
Beatrice T. Dobie (personnel); Carol Flaumenhaft
(consumer affairs); James L. Mercer (Europe/South
Pacific); Herbert Sorkin (production); Paul R. Stewart
(marketing)

WORLD WAR II

Editorial Staff for *Japan at War*
Editor: Gerald Simons
Designer/Picture Editor: Raymond Ripper
Chief Researcher: Charles S. Clark
Text Editors: Richard D. Kovar, Brian McGinn,
Robert Menaker, Henry Woodhead
Staff Writers: Donald Davison Cantlay, John Newton
Researchers: Kristin Baker, LaVerle Berry,
Kathleen Burke, Mary G. Burns, Jane Freundel Levey,
Jayne T. Wise, Paula York
Art Assistant: Mikio Togashi
Editorial Assistant: Connie Strawbridge

Special Contributors
Champ Clark, David S. Thomson (text);
Hiromi Koyama, Michael McCaskey (translation)

Editorial Production
Production Editor: Douglas B. Graham
Operations Manager: Gennaro C. Esposito,
Gordon E. Buck (assistant)
Assistant Production Editor: Feliciano Madrid
Quality Control: Robert L. Young (director),
James J. Cox (assistant), Daniel J. McSweeney,
Michael G. Wight (associates)
Art Coordinator: Anne B. Landry
Copy Staff: Susan B. Galloway (chief), Allan Fallow,
Victoria Lee, Barbara F. Quarmby, Celia Beattie
Picture Department: Betty Hughes Weatherley
Traffic: Jeanne Potter

Correspondents: Elisabeth Kraemer (Bonn); Margot
Hapgood, Dorothy Bacon, Lesley Coleman (London);
Susan Jonas, Lucy T. Voulgaris (New York);
Maria Vincenza Aloisi, Josephine du Brusle (Paris);
Ann Natanson (Rome). Valuable assistance was
provided by Ed Reingold, Bureau Chief, Tokyo.
The editors also wish to thank: Judy Aspinall,
Karin B. Pearce, Millicent D. Trowbridge (London);
Carolyn T. Chubet, Miriam Hsia, Christina
Lieberman (New York); Mimi Murphy (Rome);
Lawrence Chang (Taipei); S. Chang, Akio Fujii,
Eiko Fukuda, Shoichi Imai, Frank Iwama, Susumu
Naoi, Miwa Natori, Katsuko Yamazaki (Tokyo);
Shinkichi Natori (Yokohama).

The Consultants: COLONEL JOHN R. ELTING, USA (Ret.),
is a military historian and author of *The Battle of
Bunker's Hill, The Battles of Saratoga* and *Military
History and Atlas of the Napoleonic Wars.* He edited
*Military Uniforms in America: The Era of the Ameri-
can Revolution, 1755-1795* and *Military Uniforms in
America: Years of Growth, 1796-1851,* and was asso-
ciate editor of *The West Point Atlas of American Wars.*

H. CARROLL PARISH, a veteran of the U.S. Navy in the
battle for Okinawa and the Occupation of Japan, has
taught government and diplomatic history at Waseda
University in Japan. A former dean at the University of
California, Los Angeles, he is one of the founders of
the Associated Japan-America Societies of the United
States and serves as Chairman of the Japan-America
Society of Southern California.

KOICHI KAWANA was drafted while a teenager during
the War to work in an airplane-parts plant at Op-
pama, Japan. He graduated from Yokohama Municipal University, and won a scholarship to the University of California, Los Angeles, where he now lectures
in Japanese art, architecture and landscape design.

Library of Congress Cataloguing in Publication Data

Time-Life Books.
  Japan at war.

  (World War II; v. 26)
  Bibliography: p.
  Includes index.
    1. World War, 1939-1945—Japan.
2. Japan—History—1912-1945. I. Title. II. Series.
D767.2.T5 1980   940.53'52   80-24612
ISBN 0-8094-2528-9
ISBN 0-8094-2527-0 (lib. bdg.)
ISBN 0-8094-2526-2 (retail ed.)

For information about any Time-Life book, please write:

Reader Information
Time-Life Books
541 North Fairbanks Court
Chicago, Illinois 60611

CHAPTERS

PICTURE ESSAYS

CONTENTS

THE ROAD TO PEARL HARBOR

Lieut. Colonel Kanji Ishihara (center), an instigator of Japanese military expansion, visits Manchuria in 1932 after it had become the puppet state of Manchukuo.

TWO DECADES OF PATRIOTIC VIOLENCE

For Japan, the two decades that followed World War I were a tumultuous time of social and economic crisis, augmented by a series of natural disasters *(left)*. Through those years, the nation was steadily propelled toward a new world war by a small but relentless group of militant nationalists. These men, many of them ambitious Army officers, proposed to solve Japan's problems by expansion abroad and by reform at home, purging the country of its borrowed Western ways.

The Japanese had staked their future on adapting useful Western institutions. Beginning in about 1880, they had industrialized in record time and had created the Diet, their version of a Western parliament. But to the superpatriots, such imports meant the death of Japanese traditions. So they inveighed against the Diet, arguing that it had sundered the mystical union between the people and the Emperor. And they called for the abolition of elections and political parties; these "evils of imported democracy" they said, prevented the realization of that ideal condition, "a national opinion in which no dissenting voice is heard."

As the hard-line nationalists demanded, Japan sought colonies on the Asian mainland; these would supply much-needed raw materials, provide a captive market for Japanese manufactured goods and serve as an outlet for the nation's surplus population. But Japanese expansion prompted punitive embargoes by Western nations, and this in turn stirred bitter resentment among the nationalists. Said one: "Just as Japan was getting really good at the game of grab, the other powers, who had all they wanted, suddenly got an excess of virtue and called the game off."

Through all of this, jingoists were preaching violence as the best means to achieve political ends. "Stab, stick, cut and shoot," exhorted one fanatic. "The flames will start and fellow idealists will join." He was right. Assassination and mutiny dramatized the superpatriots' cause and fostered a national consensus for a war of conquest. By 1941, newspapers were trumpeting the nationalists' line: "Peace and contentment can be gained only by eradicating the evil encroachment of the Anglo-Saxons."

A survivor stands forlornly amid the ruins of a rural spinning mill destroyed by an earthquake, one of dozens that ravaged Japan in the 1920s.

Nervous citizens queue up behind police lines to withdraw their savings from a Tokyo bank during a financial panic that caused 37 bank failures in 1926.

Peasant girls, sold into prostitution by their fathers, bring their belongings to a Tokyo hostel after their deliverance by social workers.

Starving farmers and their sons strip soft bark from pine trees for food after their crops had failed in a year of drought and cold.

A NATION RIPE FOR REVOLUTION

The Great Depression struck Japan early and hard. When the bottom fell out of the Japanese economy in the mid-1920s, the entire social fabric of the nation threatened to unravel. Although the wealthy big businessmen scarcely felt the impact of the Depression, millions of people at the base of Japan's social pyramid lived and died in dreadful squalor.

By 1926, more than three million industrial workers had lost their jobs and had no place to turn except to ineffective government welfare and employment bureaus. Many others had lost their life's savings in the bank failures that followed the Tokyo earthquake of 1923.

Huge numbers of rural people, who had come to the cities to work, began a reverse migration. They found that conditions in the country were even worse. The government's anti-inflationary policy of importing cheap rice from Taiwan and Korea had made it unprofitable to grow rice domestically. Moreover, the cost of farm supplies had skyrocketed, and crop yields were seriously reduced by repeated droughts and cold weather.

Farmers' wives and daughters, who normally supplemented their families' hand-to-mouth existence by earning wages in silk mills, were left without work in 1929 when the United States, itself plunging toward the Depression, stopped purchasing Japan's silk. Farm families were now destitute, surviving on a diet of roots and tree bark. They died by the thousands from malnutrition, influenza and tuberculosis.

In city and country alike, privation led to desperation and protest. For the first time in Japan's long history, the country teetered on the verge of a popular revolt.

Beribboned Tokyo Municipal Employment Bureau officials launch a campaign to find jobs for factory workers in the late 1920s.

CRUSHING THE THREAT FROM THE LEFT

While a succession of cautious governments in Tokyo groped about unimaginatively for remedies for Japan's failing economy and appalling social inequities, radical movements on the left and the right competed in city streets and country towns for the support of the people. On one subject both factions agreed: Their nation was in need of immediate and drastic reform.

From the beginning, the rightists enjoyed one clear-cut advantage: Karl Marx and his disciples had not been Japanese. When, amid interminable workers' strikes and squabbling between tenant farmers and landlords, the ultranationalist leader Heigo Asahi leveled the charge that "foreign thought contrary to our national polity has moved in like a rushing torrent," he struck a responsive chord within the Japanese power structure.

To the elder statesmen who advised the Emperor, to the financial barons who ran

White-clad police roam threateningly through a meeting of the recently formed All-Japan Masses Party, a leftist coalition of farmers and laborers. The party was quashed by the government in only four months.

During a May Day rally held in Tokyo in 1930, a marshal wearing an arm band tries to direct a crowd of angry workers, some of them waving outlawed Red Flags, as their demonstration surges through the street.

Japan's huge family conglomerates, to the politicians financed by and closely allied with big business and to the generals who dominated the Army high command, anything that smelled of Communism was an anathema. Thus the Diet, Japan's two-house parliament, passed the Public Peace Preservation Law of 1925, authorizing the police to suppress "dangerous ideologies" and to smash organizations that "aimed to revolutionize the country."

An independent force called the *tokko* a Japanese acronym for "special high police"—was given the mandate to carry out the new law. The *tokko*, made up largely of judo experts with reputations for cruelty, enthusiastically began cracking the heads of Japanese Communists, as well as those of anyone who acted or sounded like a Communist.

The *tokko* campaign became an overwhelming success. In 1927, the Communists had been able to attract thousands of demonstrators to May Day rallies staged in the industrial centers of Tokyo, Osaka and Kobe. The following year, however, after the special police had rounded up 1,600 members of the party in a single day and permanently detained party leaders, the May Day turnout was reduced to a hard core of partisans, and the back of the Communist movement was broken. Attempts by groups of farmers and laborers to establish socialist alliances within the Japanese political system also were brutally smashed.

Untouched by the *tokko* were the many right-wing ultranationalist societies. They flourished as the Communists waned.

Japanese newsmen survey the section of Manchurian railroad where the bomb went off that triggered Japan's attack on Chinese troops. The explosion did so little damage that a train traveled the track half an hour later.

Japanese foot soldiers march smartly into a walled city in southern Manchuria in 1932 while a Japanese cameraman (foreground) films the event for theater audiences at home.

FOREIGN POLICY BY ARMY TAKE-OVER

At 10:30 p.m. on September 18, 1931, a Japanese train pulled to a halt in front of a Chinese barracks outside Mukden, a walled city in southern Manchuria. An explosion touched off by Japanese soldiers ripped the air. Nearby units of Japan's Kwantung Army, the force that had been posted to Manchuria in 1905 to protect Japanese interests acquired from the Russians in the Russo-Japanese War, sprang into action. Claiming that the Chinese had sabotaged their railway, they stormed the barracks and surged into Mukden. In a series of similar swift raids, Japanese troops routed Chinese garrisons up and down the rail line.

The officer behind the Japanese coup was Lieut. Colonel Kanji Ishihara. Ishihara had been worried that his government's recent policy of retrenchment might cause Manchuria to be handed over to China's virulently anti-Japanese regime. He fervently believed that Japanese expansion in Manchuria was the solution to Japan's dire internal problems, and this conviction had inspired him to invent a pretext for seizing Chinese territory.

The Japanese general staff welcomed Ishihara's initiative, promoted him to full colonel and allowed the Kwantung Army to capture all of Manchuria, the neighboring province of Jehol and a slice of Inner Mongolia to boot. By March 1932, the newly acquired territories had been incorporated into a puppet state called Manchukuo—Land of the Manchus. A cooperative Chinese, surrounded by Japanese advisers, was made the figurehead emperor.

According to Ishihara's dream, Manchukuo was to be "a realm of righteous rule" in which Chinese, Korean, Manchu and Mongol would thrive under Japanese leadership. In practice, however, the new territory and its people were cynically exploited by Japanese businessmen who saw the take-over as the long-sought cure for Japan's economic troubles.

What the Japanese public hailed as a just triumph, the rest of the world saw as pure aggression. The United States refused to recognize the supposedly independent state of Manchukuo, and condemned Japan for violating international agreements. The League of Nations ordered a commission under the British Lord Lytton to investigate.

The commission laid the blame squarely on the Japanese, and the League approved its report by a 42-to-1 vote (Japan casting the only "nay"). Thereupon Japan withdrew from the League.

"It is the holy mission of Japan to establish peace in the Orient," proclaimed the War Minister, General Sadao Araki. "The League of Nations does not respect this mission. The siege of Japan by the whole world was revealed by the Manchurian Incident," Araki concluded. "The day will come when we will make the world look up to our national virtues."

PURIFICATION BY ASSASSINATION

Mortally wounded in the stomach, Prime Minister Hamaguchi is rushed from Tokyo Railroad Station.

Hamaguchi's assassin, the ultranationalist Tameo Sagoya, is taken into custody by police officials.

On the 14th of November, 1930, Prime Minister Osachi Hamaguchi (left) was fatally wounded on the platform of the Tokyo Railway Station by a youthful member of an ultranationalist gang. So began two years of what a Japanese statesman called "a period of brainless patriotism," during which right-wing zealots tried to "purify" Japan by murdering its leaders.

Hamaguchi's crime, in the extremists' view, was his "humiliating" acceptance of the terms of the London Naval Disarmament Conference seven months earlier, at which Japan had agreed to limit its construction of capital ships to three tons for every five tons allowed both the British and the Americans.

Early in 1932, a different faction of superpatriots struck. The Blood Brotherhood, a small band of poor farmers and fishermen organized by Nissho Inoue (right), a Shinto priest, marked 11 political and financial leaders for death. On February 7, Finance Minister Junnosuke Inoue, a dogged opponent of military expansion, was shot as he stepped from his automobile. In March, Baron Takuma Dan, the president of the powerful Mitsui conglomerate, was murdered in downtown Tokyo.

The two murders led to the arrest of the entire gang before they were able to carry out the rest of their executions. But their trial galvanized the nation. To the masses, the killers resembled the samurai of olden times—warriors who were prepared to sacrifice themselves for the good of Japan.

On May 15, while the trial of the Blood Brotherhood was attracting national attention, a group of nine young Army and Navy officers aided by right-wing civilians attempted their own coup. They failed, but not before they had murdered Prime Minister Tsuyoshi Inukai, a critic of Japanese aggression in Manchuria.

Again the public sympathized with the assassins, and their trials provided a perfect stage for ultranationalist propaganda. War Minister Araki called them "irrepressible patriots" and 110,000 petitions for clemency, many of them written in blood, poured into the court from around the country. Nine youths volunteered to stand trial in place of the defendants, and enclosed their chopped-off little fingers as tokens of sincerity. "Do not shed tears for me," one defendant declared. "Sacrifice yourselves on the altars of reform."

The killers and their accomplices escaped with mere slaps on the wrist—jail terms that were later commuted.

NISSHO INOUE

BARON TAKUMA DAN

JUNNOSUKE INOUE

TSUYOSHI INUKAI

The funeral of Prime Minister Inukai, one of three leaders (inset) murdered in 1932, goes through Tokyo.

Their heads covered to protect their identities, 14 members of the Blood Brotherhood await trial in a Tokyo courtroom on charges of conspiracy and murder.

On duty in a Tokyo precinct, a unit of tokko police stands ready to suppress antistate activities.

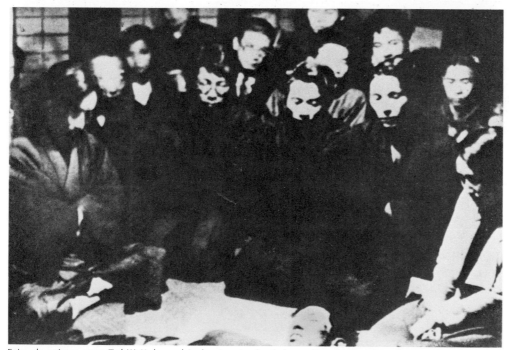

Friends grieve over Takiji Kobayashi, beaten to death by police for writing about police brutality.

Type cases litter the liberal Asahi newspaper

STAMPING OUT "UN-JAPANESE" CREEDS

"Ban views that impair national policies. Tighten controls over subversive organizations. Strengthen public unity for national mobilization."

These recommendations from War Minister Araki to Prime Minister Makoto Saito in January 1934 initiated a massive crackdown by the government against everything "un-Japanese"—this in effect meant anyone who dared to oppose Japanese military expansion in China or who criticized the cult of the Emperor. In order to justify this suppression of civil liberties, Saito obligingly declared a *hijoji*—a time of national emergency.

The military police, beefed up with a new Thought Control Bureau, were assigned to help the *tokko* implement Araki's policies. The Ministry of Education was ordered to set up a Student Control Section. Liberal and leftist publications were banned. Books, magazines and newspapers appeared with half their pages blotted out. Persons suspected of distributing seditious literature were detained indefinitely. Those with liberal views lost their jobs. Ul-

printing plant, wrecked by right-wing soldiers.   *Wanisaburo Deguchi, leader of the Omotokyo cult, is taken into custody by a policeman in 1935.*

tranationalist thugs accosted dissenters in the street and beat them up.

Other targets for the police were the many new religious cults that had attracted throngs of converts during the Depression years. In December 1935, some 500 policemen stormed the sprawling headquarters of the Omotokyo, the largest of the new cults, which had 100,000 followers. In all, the police dynamited more than 100 buildings, destroyed 50,000 religious books and arrested 300 believers.

That same year, Dr. Tatsukichi Minobe, a respected professor of Constitutional law, was accused of treason by an ultranationalist member of the Diet. Minobe's interpretation of the Constitution held that the Emperor was a representative of the people, just as the Diet was. This view was far from radical; it had been widely accepted for some 20 years. Nevertheless, Minobe was barred from teaching on grounds of lese majesty.

Superpatriotic military leaders pressured the Prime Minister into publicly disavowing Minobe's view. The Diet then passed a resolution declaring: ''The Emperor and the nation are as one body, and this national polity, perfect like a golden vase, is a tradition that goes back 3,000 years.''

Ikki Kita, the radical nationalist whose preachings about the reconstruction of Japan influenced the rebel officers, was executed in 1937 for allegedly fomenting the mutiny.

Soldiers, some of them still wearing the white headbands that signified their determination to succeed, return to their barracks after their mutiny had fizzled.

AN ARMY COUP D'ÉTAT THAT FIZZLED

At dawn on February 26, 1936, a force of 1,400 radical Army officers and men split up into groups and fanned out through the streets of Tokyo. Swiftly the soldiers seized the War Ministry, the Diet buildings, the police headquarters and the Prime Minister's residence.

One group of mutineers burst into the home of Finance Minister Korekiyo Takahashi and shot and slashed him to death. Another group pumped 47 bullets into Makoto Saito, the Lord Keeper of the Privy Seal. Still a third group hunted down and stabbed to death General Jotaro Watanabe, the moderate Inspector General of the Army. The Prime Minister, Keisuke Okada, escaped being killed only because the soldiers mistook his brother-in-law for him: While Okada hid in a maid's closet, his brother-in-law was shot.

The young officers, who had been inspired by the fierce exhortations of jingoist Ikki Kita (opposite), hoped the killings would trigger a spontaneous uprising that in turn would justify a nationwide takeover by the Army. "Our country is on the verge of war with Russia, China, Britain and America," read the mutineers' mani-festo. "Unless we rise now and annihilate the disloyal creatures who obstruct the course of true reform, the Emperor's prestige will fall to the ground."

For four days, the mutineers controlled the buildings they had captured and kept the capital paralyzed. Senior Army leaders vacillated, uncertain whether to join the rebellion or to suppress it.

Then the rebels received an order from the Imperial Palace itself to return to their barracks. They complied, anticipating a show trial and forgiveness. Instead, 123 of the officers and noncoms were tried before secret courts-martial, and 17 men, including Ikki Kita, were executed.

Prime Minister Okada (right) stands beside his brother-in-law, whom the rebels killed by mistake.

JOTARO WATANABE   MAKOTO SAITO   KOREKIYO TAKAHASHI

These Japanese leaders paid with their lives for advocating international cooperation and lower military spending.

General Hisaichi Terauchi, the War Minister, angrily denies charges against the Army in the Diet.

Moderate leader Kunimatsu Hamada feared the military's rising control over Japan's political process.

THE LAST GASPS OF FREEDOM

Shortly after the abortive mutiny of February 1936, the Army high command tried to take advantage of the government's instability by submitting a proposal to the Prime Minister to curtail the powers of the Diet. In January of 1937, the politicians counterattacked.

Kunimatsu Hamada, a respected former President of the House, accused the Army of destroying freedom of speech, scheming to usurp civil power, condoning assassination, and causing high taxation by its huge military expenditures in China.

In response, the War Minister, General Hisaichi Terauchi, accused Hamada of an unsupported insult, which could be righted only by committing suicide. Hamada retorted: "Examine the record! If you find insulting words there, I shall apologize by committing suicide. If there are no such words, you should commit suicide."

Neither of the men took his own life, but War Minister Terauchi resigned in protest and the government collapsed. In the ensuing elections, the moderate candidates lost ground in both houses of the Diet. Then the simmering conflict with China over the Japanese conquest of Manchuria broke out into full-scale war. The Army quickly prepared a National Mobilization Bill giving sweeping powers to the government, including absolute control over industry, labor and the press. The Diet meekly voted its approval.

In February 1940, Diet member Takao Saito made one final, courageous effort to halt the Army's policy of expansion. He branded the war with China as nothing but aggression cloaked in self-righteous language. "If we miss a chance for peace," Saito declared, "the politicians of today will be unable to erase their crime even by their deaths."

The military was incensed. Saito was hauled before a Diet disciplinary committee and ordered to resign. Six months later, all political parties in Japan were banned.

Takao Saito, an antimilitary member of the Diet, blasts Japan's China policy on February 2, 1940. Saito's speech was the last public criticism of the Army.

TOASTING AN ALLIANCE OF CONVENIENCE

Events in Western Europe in the spring and summer of 1940 convinced Japan's military leaders and their civilian allies that Tokyo should join the Rome-Berlin Axis without delay. Hitler's victorious sweep to the sea had suddenly created a power vacuum in Southeast Asia, tempting Japan to move in on British and Dutch possessions there. If Japan and Germany became allies, argued the expansionists, the Germans would leave Asia to the Japanese.

In Berlin, Ambassador Hiroshi Oshima lobbied vigorously with the Nazi hierarchy. At home, the ultranationalists mobilized civilians and soldiers to campaign for the partnership. The public, conditioned to blaming the United States and Britain for Japan's woes, was easily won over.

Hitler and Mussolini welcomed the alliance as a means of neutralizing the United States, and on September 27, 1940, Japan, Germany and Italy signed the Tripartite Pact, pledging to "assist each other by all political, economic and military means." Japan's militarists had once again won a victory at home, and they immediately began planning a campaign of conquest in Southeast Asia and the Southwest Pacific. The onslaught would begin with an air attack calculated to destroy the United States Pacific Fleet at its home base: Pearl Harbor.

War Minister Hideki Tojo (center) and Foreign Minister Yosuke Matsuoka (second from right) join

Japanese, German and Italian officials in a toast to the 1940 Tripartite Pact. Ironically, the Axis powers negotiated the treaty in English to simplify translation.

1

THE SPIRIT OF JAPAN

From behind the yawning moat and forbidding walls of an old Tokyo fortress where a gentle sovereign now resided, there issued forth on a brilliant December morning in 1941 an Imperial Rescript of War sonorous in its ceremonial phrasing and laden with fearful portent for the Japanese Empire and for the world:

> We, by grace of heaven, Emperor of Japan, seated on the Throne of a line unbroken for ages eternal, enjoin upon you, Our loyal and brave subjects: We hereby declare war on the United States of America and the British Empire.
>
> The hallowed spirits of Our Imperial Ancestors guarding Us from above, We rely upon the loyalty and courage of Our subjects in Our confident expectation that the task bequeathed by Our forefathers will be carried forward, and the sources of evil will be speedily eradicated.

This declaration of war was broadcast at 11:40 a.m. on December 8 (Tokyo time), about four hours after Japanese planes had attacked the United States Pacific Fleet at Pearl Harbor. The imperial rescript had been written not by the Japanese Emperor, Hirohito, but by the advisers who lived in his shadow and who dictated policy through his mystic authority. In tragic irony, the commitment to war had been made against the wishes and judgment of the Emperor himself, whose reign had been assigned the descriptive name *Showa*—Enlightened Peace.

The rescript made official the earlier radio news that had stunned many of the 73 million people in Japan proper (100 million throughout the Empire). That morning, the Japanese who bought their newspapers at Tokyo's Shimbashi railroad station "took three steps, stopped suddenly to read better, inclined their heads, then recoiled," reported French journalist Robert Guillain. "They raised faces that had become impenetrable, transformed into masks. Not a word to the vendor, not a word exchanged among themselves."

Kiyoshi Togasaki, a newspaper editor in Tokyo, had been more aware than most people that Japan stood at the brink of war with the West. Still, the coming of hostilities took him aback. "I didn't believe it was possible at the time," Togasaki said later. "The general public was not prepared. It came all of a sudden." Junpei Gomikawa, a steel-company researcher who was familiar with the comparative production capacities of Japan and the United States, recalled: "For me, it was as if the heavens shook and the earth trembled." Said Yoko Matsuoka, a young Tokyo housewife: "Pearl Harbor was just as jolting to the Japanese as it must have been to the Americans."

The people of Japan had ample reason to be apprehensive. For more than four years the nation had been mired in a costly war against China. More than 188,000 Japanese had already been killed, the country's precarious economy had been severely drained, and rationing of rice and other staples was in force. Now, in addition to that cancerous conflict, Japan was staking its fate against the Anglo-American powers it had for so long emulated and envied, admired and hated.

Compounding the awful challenge of war with the West was the fact that the Japanese home islands possessed virtually none of the natural resources necessary for the waging of war. Even though Japan would soon acquire vital raw materials by conquering rich enemy colonies in Asia and the Pacific, Japanese war production could not conceivably match that of the United States over a prolonged period. Clearly, Japan must defeat the Americans soundly before U.S. armament factories could gear up: Therefore Japanese planning called for a short war. Japanese forces would fan out in a defensive line and permit the U.S. to attack in vain until the Americans lost heart and quit the war, leaving Japan with its newly conquered empire.

Yet even within the small circle of military and civilian leaders who were privy to the plans, some officials held out little hope for such a smashing victory. Earlier in the year the Emperor, recalling the 1905 naval battle in which Japan had routed czarist Russia, asked the Imperial Navy's Chief of Staff, Admiral Osami Nagano, "Will you win a great victory? Like the Battle of Tsushima?" Replied Nagano: "I am sorry, but that will not be possible." Said Emperor Hirohito: "Then the war will be a desperate one."

It surely would. But in conceiving and embarking on their perilous adventure, Japan's leaders were counting on a hidden force. The imperial rescript had transcended rhetoric. To the Emperor's subjects, believing as they did that the words came from a direct descendant of the sun goddess Amaterasu, the rescript carried not only the force of secular law but the sanction of divine inspiration. Reaching deep into the mists of legend, the Emperor's declaration of war summoned strength from a source deemed far more powerful than any hardware that might roll off Western assembly lines. It was called *Yamato damashii*—the Spirit of Japan.

Although the phrase defied precise definition, Japanese leaders were utterly convinced that their nation's people were endowed with a spiritual strength that would prevail over superior manpower and material resources. In the end, they were proved wrong. Yet to an incredible degree throughout the War, the Spirit of Japan was indeed a driving, sustaining force.

Japan was united as no other nation in World War II. The dedicated sailors who begged for the privilege of steering torpedoes to certain extinction and the young airmen who hurtled to deliberate self-destruction as Kamikaze pilots were the natural products of their nation's educational, military and religious traditions and training. For the sake of nation and Emperor, an emotional people submitted virtually without murmur to a regimentation that reached from the lofty and austere office of Prime Minister Hideki Tojo down to the city block and the rural rice paddy. Japan was barren ground for political dissidents, and dissidence included not only deeds, not only words, but even the harboring of "dangerous thoughts."

Japan's war was total war. The Japanese people stoically endured slow starvation. Women wielded picks in coal mines, children worked long hours in factories, old men dug pine roots to make a crude fuel, and even Buddhist monks were conscripted for military service. Almost one million Japanese civilians perished in hundreds of bombing raids, yet near the end hundreds of thousands of citizens would prepare, with no weapons except sharpened sticks, to fight off an enemy invasion.

Such were the manifestations of *Yamato damashii*. It was a spirit that had grown out of the history of the Japanese nation and its people.

Exactly when and whence the Japanese people came is lost in folklore and contrived legend. But sometime before the Christian era there was a steady and burgeoning migration of basically Mongolian peoples who passed down the Korean peninsula, beat their way across the straits and made landfall on the volcanic archipelago that rises off East Asia. Mixing with the people they found there, they settled on the three southernmost islands; the islands had a total land area slightly larger than that of Italy, with no spot more than 70 miles from the sea. The migrants lived in the majestic presence of mountains towering on every side, in the green valleys and on the wooded slopes of a land blessed by a temperate climate and an abundance of sweet water, but cursed by a dearth of mineral riches.

The Japanese who went to war with the West in 1941 were, with scarcely any dilution of stock, direct descendants of those primitive tribesmen; of the nation's wartime population, less than 1 per cent was of other extraction. Joined in common culture and outlook, isolated by geography and at times by political decree, the Japanese were perhaps the most homogeneous of the world's major peoples.

Though centuries of Japanese history were marked by swift and sometimes violent change, certain conditions and values remained constant. By reason of climate and topography (less than 20 per cent of Japan's land is level enough for cultivation), a system of wet-field rice farming prevailed almost unchanged from the Second Century into the 20th. In tens of thousands of tiny patches averaging 2.5 acres apiece, peasants shared the labor and benefits of the community irrigation networks that watered the grain on which their lives depended.

From that profound sharing emerged a communal view of life—a sense, rising above ancient clan or subsequent feudal fief, that their vital interests must be served by cooperation and mutual understanding. As Japan grew into the most densely populated nation on earth, the Japanese came to live in groups, play in groups, do business by groups and be governed by consensus. Dissension was impractical.

Owing so much to so little available land, the Japanese felt a deep gratitude to nature and a keen appreciation of its beauties. This reverence evolved into a polytheism in which natural phenomena were personified and deified. The sun goddess was central; but innumerable natural wonders—a wind-swept tree, a dainty flower, a sparkling stream, an insect with gossamer wings—were venerated in shrines sprinkled throughout Japan.

The indigenous religion became known as Shinto—the Way of the Gods. In its pure and simple form, Shinto offered not a code for moral conduct but rituals for celebrating the miracles of nature. In the 1920s and 1930s, it became the Japanese state religion and was transformed into an instrument for nationalism that became increasingly potent as World War II approached.

Since the gods of Shinto assumed human form, it was perhaps inevitable that great men would be revered as more than human. Godly lineage was attributed to the leading family of a tribal group that emerged in the Sixth Century as the dominant power of western Japan. According to epic chronicles, the god Izanagi and the goddess Izanami gave birth to the Japanese islands, and then Izanagi, by the peculiar process of washing his nose and his eyes, produced the sun goddess Amaterasu and her wild brother Susanowo, god of the storm. Susanowo was jealous of Amaterasu and plagued her so unmercifully that she withdrew into a cave, and darkness fell upon the world.

This condition was of course inconvenient to all. Other gods and goddesses gathered outside the cave and created a sacred tree in whose branches they placed a mirror—which later became part of the regalia of Japan's Emperors. One goddess performed a provocative dance, arousing so much enthusiasm that Amaterasu peeked out of the cave to see

One and a half hours after the Japanese surprise attack on Pearl Harbor in 1941, Colonel Hideo Ohira (top) of the Imperial Headquarters reads the announcement of war with the United States and Great Britain to an assembly of newsmen. Shortly afterward, stunned citizens of Tokyo (bottom) stop on the street to hear the news broadcast on the radio.

30

what was happening. Spying her own image in the mirror, she was lured far enough from her hiding place to be drawn out completely by one of the gods. And lo, there was light.

Susanowo was exiled from heaven for his bad behavior, and took up residence on Honshu, largest of the Japanese islands. But he made amends to Amaterasu by presenting her with a sword—which also took its place in the imperial regalia. The myth suggests that Susanowo and his progeny were the first inhabitants of Japan and the forebears of the Japanese people. As for Amaterasu, her grandson Ninigi-no-Mikoto was designated to rule over Japan, and it was Ninigi's great-grandson Jimmu who became the nation's first Emperor. When Hirohito assumed his throne on December 25, 1926, he became the 124th Emperor in a line that could be traced with fair accuracy back to Jimmu.

To the early Japanese, it was quite acceptable that the line was often kept alive by extramarital unions; Emperor Hirohito's own father was the son of the Emperor Meiji and a lady of the court. It was essential, however, that the Emperor have the closest possible blood relationship to his predecessor, for he was the trunk of a heavenly tree, and the Japanese people were its branches. Hirohito was far from convinced of his divine origins and sacred authority, but he thoroughly understood that the Amaterasu myth made him the symbolic father of Japan's national family, for whom Japanese soldiers would give their lives.

Sometime after Jimmu's line had been established, the office of Emperor was relegated to a titular position. In 645 A.D. a family led by Kamatari Fujiwara gained dominance over what passed for Japanese government—and Japan entered into almost 400 years of shadow administration and seminal cultural change.

Throughout that period, the Fujiwara effectively ruled Japan, always in the name of the Emperor and always from behind the throne as regents or civil dictators. A wily breed, the family recognized the advantages of keeping the Emperor as the visible representation of hereditary authority. But they realized too that if the Emperor were to take part in the decision-making process, he would eventually be tarnished by unpopular, unwise or unsuccessful policies, his divine aura would dissipate and he would be seen as just another human, eminently capable of fallacy and folly. Thus, under the Fujiwara regime and its successors, the proper political place of the Emperor was "above the clouds," leaving the mundane problems of government to whatever group happened to dominate.

The Fujiwara developed a splendid system for maintaining their power through the Emperor. A Fujiwara maiden would be given in marriage to a young Emperor who—because being a ceremonial sovereign was such a routine and confining job—could usually be persuaded to abdicate after siring an heir. A Fujiwara would always be handy to act as regent until the child Emperor reached maturity. Then, in ceaseless cycle, another Fujiwara bride would step forth, another heir would result, another Emperor would abdicate in favor of mortal pleasures, and another Fujiwara regency would govern.

With their main islands separated from the coast of China by more than 450 miles of open sea, the early Japanese had had little contact with the highly developed culture of their neighbor. But what the first Fujiwara governors did know of China they vastly admired. And they saw in China's sophisticated T'ang Dynasty an opportunity to bring backwater Japan into the mainstream of Eastern civilization. They borrowed wholesale but, as the West later learned at huge cost, they showed a positive genius for altering borrowed ideas and techniques to suit Japanese tastes and needs.

To T'ang China traveled scholars and technicians, artists and artisans, administrators and warriors. The epitome of T'ang elegance—in poetry and painting, in architecture and landscaping, in manners and in methods—was adopted and adapted to the simpler, more naturalistic Japanese style. In a lengthy process of transliteration, the written signs of monosyllabic Chinese were borrowed and transformed into polysyllabic Japanese by the addition of invented phonetic characters.

In order to develop a highly centralized government, the Fujiwara followed the T'ang model, dividing the nation into provinces and creating a town-and-countryside administrative apparatus. Controlling the structure from the Fujiwara capital of Nara was an elaborate T'ang-type bureaucracy tailored to Japanese institutions. The bureaucrats also set up a Council of Deities, which concerned itself with the religious side of the Emperor's functions, and an Imperial Household Ministry, which was an invisible layer of government between those who held real power and the Emperor, who symbolized it.

All in all, the Fujiwara regime was benign; during one 300-year span there was not a single political execution. Within the administrative system, however, lay the germ of the Fujiwara's downfall. Members of the fecund family, along with Fujiwara allies, were dispersed throughout the provinces where, as reward for their governing services, they received tax-free lands. To supervise and maintain order on their vast estates, these territorial lords retained great numbers of armed men.

Late in the 12th Century a feud within the Fujiwara family over political patronage led to a series of savage struggles between the rival factions—and when the fighting ended the Fujiwara found that they had been supplanted in secular supremacy by their own military satraps. So began an 800-year period of military dominance in Japanese government that ended only 33 years before Hirohito's birth.

Thirty years into this militaristic period, Japan witnessed the debut of the samurai, superlative warrior-servitors who exalted the virtues of bravery, honor, self-discipline and stoic acceptance of death. The emergent samurai power was embodied in the Minamoto, a formidable fighting family, whose leader, Yoritomo, in 1192 received from a 13-year-old Emperor the title *Sei-i tai-shogun*—barbarian-subduing general. Thereafter, while the shogun government set up by the Minamoto ruled from a capital established in the seashore town of Kamakura, Japanese Emperors at Kyoto receded ever further into the mist. Although their lofty office remained as an institutional convenience, the Emperors themselves were sadly neglected; poverty forced one of them to make a living by peddling samples of his calligraphy on the streets of Kyoto.

The samurai, memorialized on scrolls as resolute figures in tinted armor, toting the swords that were their symbols of status, were the moving force of the day. Unlike their Western counterparts, the generally crude and illiterate medieval knights, the samurai felt perfectly at home with poetry, painting, calligraphy and other gentle arts. They were interested in Buddhism, the sophisticated Indian religion that had arrived in Japan from China in the Sixth Century. The samurai were especially attracted to Zen Buddhism, with its stress on loyalty and indifference to pain as essential virtues.

For all their cultural pursuits, the samurai were fighters first; they established an enduring tradition of courage—even suicidal courage. In 1274 the Mongol Emperor Kublai Khan, whose superb cavalry had scourged Eurasia from southwestern Russia to Korea, embarked on a campaign to expand his domain to Japan. An enormous armada of 450 ships first landed 15,000 soldiers on the little islands of Iki-shima and Tsushima, between Korea and Kyushu, the southernmost of Japan's main islands. Small garrisons of samurai there were exterminated, but in sacrificing their lives they cost the invaders precious time. Before the Mongols could disembark and deploy at Kyushu's Hakata Bay, the typhoon season was at hand and, in the face of threatening weather, the Mongol fleet withdrew.

Against the day of the invaders' return, the samurai built a wall along the shores of Hakata Bay and prepared themselves to perish in its defense. In 1281 the great Khan again sent forth his forces, this time 150,000 strong and armed with such fearsome modern weapons as catapult-launched gunpowder bombs. For 53 days the hopelessly outnumbered samurai frustrated all efforts by the Mongols to burst through the wall. Then, on August 14, an unseasonable typhoon shattered the Mongol armada and delivered the Japanese homeland from its darkest danger. The Japanese understandably viewed the tempest as an intervention by Providence. They called it the *Kamikaze*—or Divine Wind.

About 260 years after the Divine Wind brought salvation, another storm shaped Japan's destiny: It drove ashore some Portuguese traders, who were, so far as is known, the first Westerners to land on Japanese soil. Where Western seafarers went, Christian emissaries were sure to follow, and in 1549 a mission led by the Basque Jesuit Francis Xavier arrived on Kyushu. The Jesuits received a warm welcome, for Xavier was soon writing: "It seems to me that we shall never find among heathens another race to equal the Japanese. They are people of very good manners, good in general, and not malicious; they are men of honor to a marvel, and prize honor above all else in the world."

Yet as would be dramatically demonstrated, Christianity's foothold in Japan was highly tenuous—and the Japanese were much less interested in the new faith than they were in the fact that the early Western visitors brought with them

Dressed in the robes of Shinto priests, the city fathers of Osaka watch the sunrise on a wooded mountaintop to conclude the Shinto purification ceremony of misogi. Participation in this ancient ritual, which included exercises, prayers, bathing and flag raising, was encouraged by the government as a means of fostering Yamato damashii (the Spirit of Japan).

a weapon that changed the dimensions of samurai warfare.

The weapon was the matchlock musket, and the Japanese rapidly became adept at making and using it. The firearm played a decisive part in a decade of civil strife—from which emerged in the 1580s one of the great strongmen of Japanese history. His name was Hideyoshi Toyotomi, he was the son of a peasant, he was tiny even among a people of generally small stature, he was renowned for his ugliness, and he was exceedingly tough and smart.

Keenly conscious of his own origins, Hideyoshi set about making certain that no more upstarts could rise to power. Under the pretext of needing metal to use in building a gigantic Buddhist shrine in Kyoto, Hideyoshi confiscated all weapons held by peasants. As for Japan's aristocracy, Hideyoshi brooked no opposition. Wrote a Western missionary: "He is so feared and obeyed that, with no less ease than a father of a family disposes of the persons in his household, he rules the principal kings and lords of Japan; changing them at every moment, and stripping them of their original fiefs, he sends them into different parts, so as to allow none of them to strike root deep."

According to legend, Hideyoshi traveled to the Kamakura shrine of Yoritomo Minamoto, where he spoke to the spirit of the founder of the Minamoto shogunate: "You were of illustrious stock and not, like me, descended from peasants. But after conquering all the Empire, I mean to conquer China. What do you think of that?"

Whether or not the tale was true, Hideyoshi did launch two attempts to invade China by way of Korea—although both times he himself prudently stayed at home to consolidate his hold on the country. In the first invasion, no fewer than 200,000 Japanese fought their way northward up the Korean peninsula; they were finally repelled at the Yalu River in January 1593. Five years later, the second expeditionary force was faring poorly when, back in Japan, Hideyoshi died. Relieved by news of this event, the Japanese withdrew—not to undertake another foreign military adventure until the eve of the 20th Century.

As the power behind Japan's figurehead throne, Hideyoshi was succeeded after a brief period of turmoil by his foremost military and political follower, Tokugawa Ieyasu, whose family dynasty was to lead Japan through one of the most peculiar periods in human history. Under Tokugawa rule, the Japanese were to know some 250 years of unbro-

ken peace. Yet they paid a price beyond calculation, enduring an ironclad regimentation from which they would not be completely released until they were liberated from their own leaders at the end of World War II.

Like Hideyoshi, Tokugawa Ieyasu viewed the modest growth of Japanese Christianity with deepening apprehension. But his suspicions expanded to include all Western influences and, later, everything foreign. In 1612, he initiated a series of edicts that ultimately cut off Japan from the rest of the world.

By 1638, Tokugawa's shogun son had thrown out all but a few foreigners, had suppressed Japanese Christianity and had effectively imprisoned the Japanese in their homeland by imposing a death sentence on any traveler who attempted to leave the country or who returned from abroad. Two years later a Portuguese deputation made a final effort to persuade Japan's leaders to give up their isolationist policy. No sooner had the Portuguese landed than all but 13 of them were beheaded. The survivors were allowed to proceed to Macao with an official warning to other Westerners: "Let them think no more of us, just as if we were no longer in the world." Japan's only window on the outside was the port of Nagasaki, where Dutch and Chinese merchants were allowed to trade, but under ceaseless supervision.

Feudalism was further formalized and enforced by the Tokugawa warlords. They held one fourth of all Japanese agricultural land, and all major cities, ports and mines; they parceled out the rest to fewer than 300 feudal lords. The lords and their samurai followers constituted the highest of four feudal classes. Below them were peasants, then artisans and, at the bottom of the ladder, merchants. Between these classes, loyalty and duty mostly flowed upward. A member of a lower class could not leave the service of a superior without official permission. Humbler folk were to kneel and touch their foreheads to the ground when a lord rode by. Samurai were authorized to slay on the spot any inferior who became insolent.

The lords themselves were strictly controlled to prevent any conspiracy against Tokugawa supremacy. They were required to spend every other year attending the shogun's person in the capital established by the Tokugawa in the fishing village of Edo. (By the 18th Century, Edo had about one million inhabitants and was perhaps the biggest city in the world.) When the lords left Edo, their wives and children remained behind as the shogun's hostages. To forestall subversive activities during their enforced travels between countryside and capital, the lords were kept on specified routes, which passed through barriers open only from sunrise to sunset. During their overnight stops at inns near the barriers they were kept under close watch by armies of Tokugawa agents and spies. Lest a lord fall into league with an ambitious Emperor, the city of Kyoto, where the Imperial House continued to languish, was kept strictly off limits.

The cost of commuting, in addition to the vast expense of maintaining elaborate establishments in Edo, forced the lords and samurai to borrow money from the merchants, whom they held in contempt. In growing commercial centers such as Osaka and Edo, the merchants, in spite of bothersome restrictions placed on them by the Tokugawa regime, not only prospered but began to develop their own bourgeois life style, complete with kabuki theater and graceful entertainments by forerunners of the geisha. And it was from these lowly moneylenders that arose such 20th Century commercial and industrial giants as the family houses of Mitsui and Sumitomo.

For all its genius at repressing and isolating a people destined by geography and energy for a place among the great powers of the world, the Tokugawa shogunate could not endure forever. And on the 8th of July, 1853, the end was signaled by the appearance of four American warships in Edo Bay.

Two of the foreign vessels, each with a sailing ship in tow, were black-hulled steamers, products of the Industrial Revolution from which Japan had excluded itself. These two steamships were perhaps the first the Japanese had ever seen, and to the thousands of people who lined the shore that day they would always be remembered as the *kurofune*—the black ships.

The little flotilla was under the command of Commodore Matthew Calbraith Perry, a gruff old seadog who had distinguished himself during the Mexican War. Perry's instructions were to propose that "the United States and Japan should live in friendship and have commercial relations with each other." To achieve that felicitous goal, Perry was admonished to be "courteous and conciliatory but at the same time firm and decided." In fact, he turned out to be a skillful diplomat.

Far from certain as to what might strike the mysterious Japanese fancy, Perry came bearing a wondrous assortment of gifts—including two Audubon folios (Birds of America and Quadrupeds of America), baskets of champagne, a barrel of whiskey, a cask of Madeira, a crate of the revolvers invented and manufactured by Samuel Colt, a daguerreotype camera, a telegraph instrument, a small steam locomotive and cars, and for good measure, a cockatoo in a cage. He also carried a letter from Millard Fillmore, who had been the President of the United States when Perry set sail more than seven months before. Fillmore had addressed the letter to his "Great and Good Friend," the Emperor of Japan.

Not surprisingly, the Americans' arrival threw the Japanese into consternation. For three days Japanese officials did not even dare inform the sitting Tokugawa shogun, a man of frail health. Upon finally learning by accident of the flotilla's presence, the shogun was so distressed that he took to his bed, remaining there throughout Perry's stay.

The shogun's indisposition left the problem of dealing with the Americans to his council of elders, a body of uncertain status and precarious tenure. So perilous was council membership, in fact, that if an elder proposed an amendment to Tokugawa law that failed to be adopted, he was expected to commit ceremonial suicide. The council authorized a mobilization of some 20,000 samurai to fend off the "hairy barbarians." The fighting skills of Japan's samurai class had grown dull during the two and a half centuries of the Tokugawa peace. Nevertheless, a fully equipped army was mustered—and the price of a new suit of armor quadrupled overnight.

Since Japan's defenses were clearly no match for the firepower represented by Perry's guns, the elders adopted the best policy they could; they dithered and delayed while ordinary Japanese prayed for the coming of another Divine Wind. Perry was in no great hurry: He set off on a visit to China, leaving Fillmore's letter behind him and promising to return the next spring for a reply.

He was back in February 1854, and on March 8, near a camphor tree in a little village named Yokohama, entered into negotiations that lasted the rest of the month. The Japanese proved to be, in Perry's opinion, a "sagacious and de-

ceitful people." But on March 31 the treaty that unlocked the door to Japan was signed. Under its terms, the ports of Shimoda and Hakodate were made available to American ships for the supply of "wood, water, provisions and coal, and other articles their necessities may require." Also, an American consul took up residence at Shimoda and was able to conclude a commercial treaty with Japan in 1858. Within the next few years, those seemingly modest concessions would be greatly expanded as other nations—notably Great Britain and Russia—came crowding in and forced the Japanese to grant them similar concessions and also extraterritorial rights.

For Japan, the change was revolutionary. And since the House of Tokugawa had for so long relied upon resistance to change as its primary policy, it now began to crumble.

Clearly the shogunate had failed in its duty to provide military protection and security for Japan, its people and its Emperor. Moreover, by pushing the Imperial House still further to the sidelines of secular power, the shogun had inadvertently absolved the Emperor of all blame for the incursions begun by Perry. The shogunate was therefore fatally vulnerable to the slogan that now arose: "Honor the Emperor! Expel the barbarians!" That cry resounded primarily in western Japan, where a group of samurai banded together under the banner of the Imperial House in rebellion against the Tokugawa regime.

Their revolution was by no means quickly accomplished. In 1860, seven years after Perry's arrival, the leading member of the Tokugawa council was assassinated as he rode to the family fortress at Edo, and a Japanese writer hailed the event as the end of the shogunate, which had been set up in Kamakura in the 12th Century: "And so the prestige of the Tokugawa family, which had endured for 300 years, which had really been more brilliant than Kamakura in the age of Yoritomo on a moonlit night when the stars are shining, fell to ruin in the space of one morning."

And still the tenacious Tokugawa clung to their seat of power. The end did not come for eight years more; in 1868 the rebel forces finally seized Edo, which they soon renamed Tokyo, or Eastern Capital.

The first Emperor of the Restoration period had assumed the throne in 1867 at the age of 15; his 45-year reign—designated *Meiji,* or Enlightened Rule, after his death—would stand as Japan's golden age. The Emperor set the style for that era in the first year of his reign with his so-called Charter Oath, which enunciated the policy that would reshape Japan and dictate its destiny: "Knowledge shall be sought all over the world, and thus shall be strengthened the foundation of the imperial polity."

Where once Japan had looked to China for learning, the Meiji leaders now turned avidly toward the powerful nations of the West for their economic, political, technological and military models. Japanese of all interests and callings were sent out to study the ways of the West; beyond that, Western engineers and educators, economic and legal ex-

perts and military professionals were hired by the Meiji government and brought to Japan as instructors.

The transformation was breathtaking. By 1872 a British consular official in Tokyo could comment: "Almost in every street a certain number of shops may be seen where nothing but foreign objects are offered for sale." Japanese children played a game in which they bounced balls to the cadence of the "Civilization Ball Song," which listed the 10 Western items most desired by the Japanese: steam engines, gas lamps, cameras, telegrams, lightning rods, newspapers, schools, mailing services, steamships and hansom cabs. A British architect was brought to Japan specifically for the purpose of building an enormous ballroom—the

Baiko Onoue, as Hangan, prepares to commit seppuku with a cloth-wrapped sword.

THE NOBLEST WAY TO DIE

Many Japanese romanticized seppuku—an extremely painful act of ritual suicide that was performed by cutting open one's abdomen with a short sword. The practice dated from the Ninth Century and won acceptance 300 years later as the only way for a high-ranking samurai to remove a blot on his honor. Seppuku—known in the West as hara-kiri—survived into modern Japan largely because of a famous 18th Century drama, *Chushingura (The Tale of the Loyal Retainers),* which glorified and glamorized ritual suicide for millions of ordinary Japanese.

In the play, which was loosely based on a true story, a lord named Hangan is forced to commit seppuku for a forbidden act—drawing his sword in a Shinto shrine (to warn off a man who was making advances toward his wife). The seppuku takes place on a stage crowded with retainers and haughty officials; the performer playing Hangan kneels, makes a final speech and courageously ends his life.

So moving is the scene, and so brave and honorable is Hangan's suicide, that generations of Japanese came to believe that seppuku was the noblest way to die.

Hall of the Baying Deer—in which Japanese could practice Western dance steps.

Western change reached early into the imperial court. Electricity was installed in the Emperor's palace—although it was not used for a long time out of fear that the place might be consumed by fire. Ladies of the court were encouraged to speak out in the forthright fashion of Western women rather than whisper behind decorously raised hands. The men of the court tried to imitate Western dress. That effort, however, was the object of amused scorn from a visiting Englishwoman: "Almost all the garments were ready-made and far too large for their wearers. Trousers were pushed at their extremities into elastic-sided boots. Ruffled top hats were pulled down over the owners' ears, or alternatively worn jauntily on the back of the head."

In emulating the West, the Meiji leaders were interested almost exclusively in external forms; they simply did not understand Western values. They wished above all else to earn respect for Japan as an equal and for the Japanese as a progressive people. As it seemed that a constitutional government would win Western regard, the Meiji oligarchy set out to create one—in a distinctly Japanese manner.

In 1881 the Emperor announced that Japan would be given a constitution soon—sometime within the next decade. A Japanese mission, headed by Hirobumi Ito, a resolute conservative among the Meiji advisers, was sent to Europe to study the constitutional systems existing there. Ito naturally spent most of his time in Germany, where he met and was mightily impressed by the Iron Chancellor, Otto von Bismarck. He also fell under the spell of the German jurist Rudolf von Gneist, who held that a constitution should not cater to democratic whims but must instead be firmly anchored to national traditions.

Ito liked what he heard, and he took the Prussian Constitution for Japan's model. He had no qualms about rejecting the more democratic examples of the United States, France and Great Britain. Ito later wrote, "I believe I have rendered an important service to my country, and I feel inwardly that I can die a happy man."

For Ito and his colleagues, the objective was to redeem their pledge to restore the Emperor to his place of highest honor, even while continuing to deny him real power. The Japanese Constitution, adopted in 1889, did just that. It revived the ancient myth of the Emperor's divine descent, glorifying him as "sacred and inviolate," and as having sprung from a line "unbroken for ages eternal" (a phrase quoted in Hirohito's Imperial Rescript of War). Yet at the same time, the Constitution made it quite clear that whatever legislation the Emperor might initiate would be invalid without the approval of the Diet.

The Diet, or parliament, was made up of an elected House of Representatives and a House of Peers whose members came from Japan's elite. The inner circle was most unwilling, however, to turn over its power either to the Japanese masses or to their elected representatives. The electorate was limited to about 6 per cent of the population—roughly the proportion of the old samurai class—and the House of Peers, in practice, was able to veto legislation propounded by the lower house.

This semblance of democracy satisfied the West. Only four years after the Constitution took effect, Great Britain showed its approval by renouncing the extraterritorial rights it had held in Japan since shortly after Perry's visit. The other Western nations soon followed suit.

In their considerable wisdom, the Emperor's advisers realized that success or failure in their desperate effort to catch up with the West would in large part depend on educating the Japanese people. As early as 1872 they instituted a system of compulsory education. The program, which among other things called for the construction of 54,000 elementary schools, was carried out at a breakneck pace: From a nation whose population in 1860 was largely illiterate, Japan by the turn of the century had become by far the best-educated country in Asia, with 95 per cent of its citizens able to read and write.

Yet as with all else, education was given a peculiarly Japanese twist. An imperial rescript issued in 1890 enunciated a fundamental code of ethics for the entire nation. Thus given the status of holy writ, it guided Japan into and through the Second World War.

Addressed to people "ever united in loyalty and filial piety," the Imperial Rescript on Education called upon the Emperor's subjects to "advance the public good and promote common interests," and to "respect the Constitution and observe the laws." Then came the ringing admonishment that would obligate a heeding people to fight a conflict impossible to win: "Should any emergency arise, offer yourselves courageously to the State; and thus guard and maintain the prosperity of Our Imperial Throne, coeval with heaven and earth."

In most other nations, it would have been just another proclamation, and a somewhat overblown one at that. But in schools throughout Japan, the reading of the Imperial Rescript on Education was accorded the significance of a religious rite. The wearing of white gloves was required for anyone who touched the scroll on which the sacred words were written. Indeed, there were cases of principals who, after accidentally dropping the document or making a mistake in its reading, atoned for their sin by committing suicide. It went without saying that in the event of fire, the resident copy of the rescript was to be rescued before anything—or anyone—else.

The entire school curriculum was shaped to promote a flaming nationalism centered on the Emperor. In required ethics courses, the ancient Shinto reverence for nature's wonders was dimmed by a militant modern Shinto in which the Japanese state and its Emperor took precedence. Regulations handed down by the Ministry of Education in Tokyo stipulated that the aim of teaching history was "to make children comprehend the fundamental character of the Empire and to foster in them the national spirit." Similarly, the object of instruction in geography was "to instill in their minds the love of their country."

Generations of Japanese school children observed the ritual of "worshipping at a distance," in which they bowed for 60 seconds each morning in the direction of the Imperial Palace. Children were also taught that if they happened to be in the assemblage during one of the Emperor's rare public appearances they must cast their eyes down to indicate their reverence for him. And each day the boys were asked by their teachers: "What is your dearest ambition?"

The answer came in a chorus of childish voices: "To die for the Emperor!"

In time, millions of them would.

To erect a bulwark against domination by Western capitalism and to create an economy that would support a military establishment, Meiji Japan stood in imperative need of heavy industry. As it had virtually none and refused foreign investment for fear of foreign control, Japan would have to start from scratch and go it alone. The manner in which the Meiji government approached its problem was one that other nations might well have noted closely.

"To study industry and overcome its difficulties," said a Meiji leader, "is a responsibility the government must assume." Dipping deeply into its own limited financial resources, which were derived mostly from an expanded land tax, the Japanese government built and operated its own factories. Entire industries sprang up, with the concentration at first on strategic military needs and only later on consumer goods. Blessed by a labor force that had been reared to look upon hard work (with low pay) as a patriotic virtue, Japan's new industrial establishment within a few years was, if not booming, at least solidly solvent.

Although the Meiji government planned to keep control of war industries, it had no intention of permanently pre-empting private enterprise. As early as 1880, the preamble to the Law on Transfer of Factories signaled a turnabout: "The factories established for encouraging industries are now well organized and business has become prosperous, so the government will abandon its ownership of factories which ought to be run by the people."

The government gradually divested itself of all but a few nonmilitary production facilities. It sold some sections at bargain rates and gave others to individuals and combines considered especially capable of managing them. The old merchant-class families were by no means the only beneficiaries; indeed, they were often deemed too cautious and set in their ways to adapt to the new industrialism. On the other hand, business-minded samurai found a new calling—if only because, as one Meiji planner put it, "with their strength of spirit nurtured through generations, the samurai are equal to any task."

The favored few who thus got in on the ground floor of Japanese industry were to become magnates of the first order, the proprietors of vast conglomerates with holdings in every segment of the Japanese economy. Collectively, they came to be called the zaibatsu—the financial clique—and their privileged relationship with the government that had spawned them was the envy of those less favored. Their success was phenomenal, and their need for raw materials by far outstripped the supply available within the little Empire. Between 1868 and 1897, imports of raw materials for Japanese factories increased fivefold. It was partly to satisfy the factories' multiplying needs that Japan undertook a policy of military aggression.

Almost without exception, the men who had led the Meiji rebellion against the Tokugawa shogunate were themselves of samurai stock. Yet as an early step in dragging Japan into the modern, Western-style world, it was clearly necessary to smash the antiquated structure of Tokugawa feudalism—of which the samurai were a basic part. Class distinctions were legally abolished and the samurai were summarily ordered to stop wearing the swords that had been sign and symbol of their superior caste. The hereditary stipend of the samurai was at first cut by one half and then terminated with one lump-sum payment. Most shocking of all in a society where for centuries only the samurai had been allowed to bear arms, a standing army was raised through universal military conscription.

Many of the samurai adapted nicely; they became part of the new industrial establishment, the backbone of government bureaucracy, the leading policemen (a profession of high prestige in Japan) and the cadre for the new army's officer corps. Others, however, were reduced to sad circumstances and found it necessary to pawn their armor and fall back on such prideful expedients as sewing pieces of white cloth inside their collars in order to give the appearance that they could afford proper underwear.

From the resentment of these unfortunates there arose in 1877 a samurai revolt that was suppressed after several months by the fledgling conscript army under General Aritomo Yamagata, an ex-samurai who might be called the father of the Japanese military. Surveying the results of his army's first major test, Yamagata pronounced himself satisfied. "The Japanese," he said, "whether of the military class or not, originally sprang from the same blood and, when

Tokyo schoolboys armed with toy rifles salute their elementary school's goshin'ei shrine, built to house a picture of the Emperor and the Empress and a copy of the revered Imperial Rescript on Education. The ceremony was intended to inculcate obedience to the Emperor.

subjected to regular discipline, could scarcely fail to make soldiers worthy of the bravery of their ancestors.''

To such leaders as Yamagata, discipline of the spirit was every bit as important as close-order drill or the manual of arms. ''An army,'' said one leader, ''does not depend on guns and ships but primarily on the feeling of patriotism.'' It was in the barracks of Meiji's reign that the word *Bushido*— the Way of the Warrior—first became widespread. Reaching deep into the Japanese past, it invoked the ancient ideals of self-discipline, loyalty toward one's superiors and fearlessness in the face of death.

As early as 1890, Yamagata drew up a plan for making

Demonstrating their patriotism, members of a Tokyo women's association parade behind Army officers in the days before the attack on Pearl Harbor. Their uniforms are the white smocks and headbands Japanese women normally wore while doing their household chores.

the Japanese Army's "direction of the future a definite one." He defined Japan's "line of sovereignty" as the nation's actual geographic frontiers. Much more ominously, he was vague about what he called a "line of interest." Wrote Yamagata: "If we wish to maintain the nation's independence and to rank among the great powers, it is necessary to step forward and defend our line of interest . . . and not be satisfied to defend only the line of sovereignty."

As it turned out, Japan's line of interest would take its soldiers and sailors far afield.

The last decade of the 19th Century and the first 40 years of the 20th Century was a time of occasional triumph and endless frustration for a Japan seeking a greater place under the sun. For the most part it was a time of Japanese militarism and vigorous colonialism.

In 1894, when Chinese troops were sent to aid Korea's King in putting down a revolt, Japan seized upon the occasion as an excuse for its own armed intervention. During a whirlwind nine-month campaign, Japanese forces expelled the Chinese from Korea and went on to capture Port Arthur and the Liaotung peninsula of southern Manchuria, the Shantung port of Wei-hai-wei and the island of Formosa. To their lasting bitterness, however, they were forced to hand back their gains—except for Formosa—under pressure from Germany, France and Russia, who then cynically divided up the spoils among themselves. It was a lesson in imperialism not soon forgotten in Tokyo.

Ten years later, in a second war over Korea, Japan stunned the world by soundly thrashing Russia both on land and at sea. America's President Theodore Roosevelt mediated a peace that recognized Japan's "permanent political, military and economic interest" in Korea. The treaty also gave Japan control of the Liaotung peninsula, together with the southern half of Sakhalin Island to the north of Japan and Russian railways in southern Manchuria from Port Arthur to Mukden. But when the Japanese were not awarded indemnities from Russia, popular indignation ran so high that crowds rioted in Tokyo's streets.

Entering World War I on the Allied side, Japan used the slaughter on the European continent to cover its own acquisition of German possessions in Shantung and in the Pacific—the Marshalls, the Carolines and the Marianas. The Versailles Peace Conference in 1919 recognized Japan's newly acquired status and territorial gains. But the Japanese were indignant when the victorious Allies refused to include in the League of Nations Covenant a Japanese amendment that would have outlawed racial discrimination. This refusal seemed to the Japanese to be another example of the irrational Occidental fear of the "yellow peril."

Japanese pride received a setback at the Washington Naval Disarmament Conference in 1922, which set a 5:5:3 ratio on battleship tonnage—with Japan coming out on the short end, behind the United States and Great Britain. But Japan was left the dominant power in the western Pacific because the United States and Britain agreed not to introduce new fortifications into the area.

In 1931, Japanese forces provoked incidents in Manchuria and overwhelmed Chinese troops in a series of rapid advances. When a League of Nations report rebuked Japan for this aggression the Japanese angrily stamped out of the League, determined to go their own way in the Far East without any regard for world opinion or for previous treaty commitments.

This reaction slowly aroused the isolationist Americans. Perceiving a threat to its interests in the Far East, the United States in 1939 renounced its commercial treaty with Tokyo and then began to curtail shipments of oil and scrap iron to Japan. The Japanese were not intimidated and by 1941 had overrun all of French Indochina. In turn the United States, joined by Great Britain and the Netherlands, imposed a total oil embargo on Japan, a devastating blow to the fuel-poor island nation. As the price for lifting the embargo, the Western nations demanded that Japan withdraw from China and Southeast Asia.

Confronted with the choice of submitting to these terms or of striking out boldly to secure its vital natural resources, Japan chose conquest, attacking Pearl Harbor, the Philippines, the Dutch East Indies and Singapore. Into the resulting conflict of World War II, Japan would pour its men, its wealth, its national energies—and its *Yamato damashii*. Said a great wartime leader: "As long as there remains the great spirit of loyalty and patriotism, we have nothing to fear in fighting America and Britain."

The speaker was Prime Minister Hideki Tojo, and within him the Spirit of Japan burned with a consuming flame.

PREPARING FOR THE BOMBERS

Wearing gas masks, Buddhist priests from Tokyo's Asakusa Temple join uniformed civil defense workers in an air-raid drill held even before Pearl Harbor.

43

"NEIGHBORHOOD LOVE IS BURNING LIKE A FLAME"

"Every home is now a battleground!" a Tokyo newspaper proclaimed on December 10, 1941, three days after Pearl Harbor. "Neighborhood love is burning like a flame." The editorial fervor celebrated Japan's *tonarigumi*, neighborhood associations that reached across barriers of class and family to involve the entire nation in civil defense.

Through 1943 and well into 1944, more than a million associations, each made up of 10 to 12 households, prepared to meet waves of U.S. bombers, even though the only air raid so far had been the minor attack on Tokyo led by Lieut. Colonel James H. Doolittle in April 1942. *Tonarigumi* members learned how to identify enemy planes, what to do during a poison-gas attack and how to dispose of incendiary bombs. Their leaders organized blackout patrols, inspected houses for fire safety and supervised the digging of trenches and home bomb shelters. They helped to raze rows of houses to make firebreaks and made sure that every family kept a rucksack of rice and medicine for emergency use.

The leaders also called practice drills incessantly, often without warning and most often at night. Attendance by at least one member of each household was mandatory, and since so many men were at the front, this person was usually a woman. Not all the women found the exercises easy or reasonable. One remembered being dismissed from a bucket brigade for spilling water: "The man in charge said, 'You're not athletic enough. Go home and send someone else.'" Another woman was disgusted by the endless repetition. "Running uphill with pails of water," she said, "seemed to me a silly and tedious way to fight a war."

But for most Japanese civilians, the air-raid drills heightened collective discipline and contributed to a sense of national unity and pride. The drills also generated false confidence, reflected in the brave words of a *tonarigumi* song:

Why should we be afraid of air raids?
The big sky is protected with iron defenses.
For young and old it is time to stand up;
We bear the honor of defending the homeland.
Come on, enemy planes. Come on many times!

Lantern-bearing tonarigumi patrols make their rounds in 1944. Many of the neighborhood air-raid wardens were men considered too old to fight.

Aircraft spotter Tsuneko Otake scans the sky for U.S. bombers during an air-raid drill. The sash she is wearing names her hometown, Kawasaki, near Tokyo.

An Army officer shows the women of a neighborhood group how to put on their gas masks correctly. He also uses diagrams to teach them how the breathing apparatus operates.

Members of the National Patriotic Women's Association make rice balls out-of-doors during an air-raid drill. The communal cookouts were intended to prepare city people for the day when enemy bombers might drive them from their homes.

Tonarigumi members clad in farm women's pants use empty buckets to put out an imaginary fire during a bucket-brigade drill. The women wore flimsy cloth hoods that were supposed to protect them from sparks.

Stretcher-bearers carry mock casualties past a model house engulfed in flames during a simulated incendiary and gas raid in Tokyo's municipal-office area.

Breathing through cloth, citizens of Tokyo run past a smoke canister during a prewar civil defense drill.

A uniformed tonarigumi leader guides his unit through a bomb-dousing drill. A flare simulates the bomb.

Working in their undershirts, students dig an air-raid trench. Their short haircuts symbolized unity with Japan's close-cropped soldiers.

Young Japanese school children attend their daily reading class, held in one of Tokyo's underground air-raid tunnels late in the War.

A crowd watches hooded firemen pull down houses in Tokyo. Some 20,000 people were relocated when their homes were razed to make firebreaks.

DIGGING TRENCHES AND BACKYARD SHELTERS

Despite the best efforts of the authorities, Tokyo's air-raid-shelter system was woefully inadequate. The trenches, dug by teams of schoolboys mobilized in 1944, did not have any seats and usually had no roofs. Tunnels were dug into the city's hillsides, but they were too far away from the residential areas to be reached in the time between the warning sirens and an attack. Although most homes had a shelter in the backyard, the typical one was a foxhole that flooded regularly from ground water or rain. "The so-called shelter," one woman wrote, "was often only a deep hole, exposed and damp."

The basements of Western-style office buildings provided ready-made protection from bombs, but such buildings were confined mostly to Tokyo's downtown district, and thus would be of little use if an air raid occurred after the workers had gone home for the night. Even if an air raid came during working hours, the city—as late as the spring of 1945—had only 18 concrete shelters, with a total capacity of fewer than 5,000 people.

When the Japanese woke up to the terrible reality of massive American bombing, it was too late.

Cloth-covered frames and draped sheets help to disguise the walls of a bank (left) and a department store during a camouflage drill held in Tokyo.

A civil defense worker holding a flag watches a canister spew a smoke screen over factories and office buildings in the business district of Tokyo.

HOPEFUL EFFORTS
TO FOOL ENEMY PILOTS

The Japanese had used camouflage during their civil defense exercises years before the outbreak of war with the United States. But their leaders' conviction that few enemy bombers would ever reach the home islands led the Japanese to ignore such deceptive tactics during the conflict. Whereas important landmarks like the Diet building were camouflaged with netting, fully 90 per cent of the office buildings in Tokyo went to war undisguised.

Ultimately, it mattered little. Camouflage, though it might have been reassuring, could hardly have protected the city from the eventual onslaught when American warplanes dropped their loads indiscriminately. Tokyo, which covered some 200 square miles, was hard to miss.

2

From his habit of riding out each morning to survey the wartime endeavors of the citizens of Tokyo, Hideki Tojo quickly became known as "the Prime Minister on Horseback." On one such foray, Tojo was dismayed to find the display stands in the great Tokyo fish market almost empty. He asked why and was told that the shortage of gasoline had reduced transport from wharf to marketplace.

"Gasoline? Gasoline!" cried the Prime Minister of Japan. "Never mind gasoline! Get up earlier!"

Simplistic solutions came naturally to the uncomplicated soldier whom the world perceived to be the virtual dictator of wartime Japan. In terms of raw personal power, Tojo was not in the same class with Adolf Hitler or Benito Mussolini; he was merely the leading representative of the shadowy clique of high-ranking Army officers who dominated Japan's government. Yet to the Japanese people—those in military uniform as well as those who toiled in the factories and the rice paddies—Hideki Tojo was the government personified and the epitome of Japanese virtues. He was strong, brave, loyal, dedicated, hard-working, forthright, generous and kind to children.

To the Allies, on the other hand, Tojo was the very soul of evil. The Western press and Allied propagandists saw him as "sinister, threatening, brutal, a Hitler with the added danger of Oriental mysticism." He was described variously as "bullet-headed Tojo" and as "beak-nosed, bald-pated Tojo," an inquisitor whose "zeal as the Heinrich Himmler of the Army," during a prewar stint as a chief of internal military security, "still clings to him like a malignant odor."

In fact, Hideki Tojo was a very ordinary man, distinguished mainly by his lineage. He was the son of a son of a samurai; his father, still in his teens when the warrior class was dispossessed of its ancient privileges, had enlisted in a noncommissioned officers' school and, 37 years later, retired from the Imperial Japanese Army as a lieutenant general. Tojo's own military career began at 15, and he had slowly risen to prominence in a succession of steady, entirely unspectacular steps that led to the position of War Minister and eventually, having been hand-picked by the Army, to the post of Prime Minister in 1941.

Tojo was 57 at the time of Pearl Harbor; he stood five feet four, weighed about 155 pounds, was almost bald and glared at the world through heavy, horn-rimmed spectacles.

TOJO AND THE TOOLS OF WAR

As an Army officer he had been known as a harsh disciplinarian, yet one who took care of his men, often reaching into his own pocket to assist them in their return to civilian life. (With that in mind, Tojo's wife once remarked that her family finances had always been "on a war footing.")

In matters military, Tojo was keen, decisive and utterly self-confident. But he was afflicted with a form of tunnel vision that let him see little outside the service in which he had spent his life. He once said that he had heard of the 1938 Munich agreement between Adolf Hitler and Britain's Neville Chamberlain but really did not know what it was all about. Asked why Europe had gone to war, Tojo replied vaguely: "As I recall it, Germany and Italy were dissatisfied with the situation then existing."

Still, what his own toil could accomplish, Tojo would achieve. "Endeavor and hard work," he told a group of Japanese students, "have been my friends throughout."

In that spirit, Tojo wore an astonishing number of official hats. Upon being named Prime Minister, he retained his portfolio as War Minister, all the while remaining an Army general on active duty. Later, as Japan's plight grew increasingly desperate, Tojo would also take on the job of Chief of Staff of the Japanese Army, thus assuming operational as well as administrative responsibilites. At various times he was Foreign Minister, relegating Japan's career diplomatic service to a place of insignificance; Home Minister, a position that put him in charge of the omnipresent police and atop a gigantic administrative pyramid built upon tens of thousands of neighborhood associations; Minister of Education, in a nation whose rigidly controlled schools were instruments of political indoctrination and military training; Minister of Commerce and Industry, responsible for industrial mobilization; and finally Munitions Minister, a post specifically created to bring about an end to the bitter and debilitating struggle for preeminence between the Japanese Army and the Japanese Navy.

In addition, Tojo worked hard at being a public personality—and thereby astonished his countrymen, who had rarely seen an important national official actually get out and mingle with the common folk. He dropped in on the markets to inquire about prices, he exhorted pilgrims to visit the great Meiji Shrine, he demanded "a far better achievement" from workers at Nagoya's Mitsubishi aircraft plant,

he put on a coal miner's head lamp and descended a 1,200-foot shaft on Kyushu to appeal to the miners for higher production. On horseback one day near his Tokyo home, he came across schoolboys dressed in khaki and toting wooden rifles. Asked Tojo: "What time do you start drilling?"

One of the boys snapped to attention and answered smartly: "Eight o'clock, General."

Tojo nodded. "And your mother," he asked, "what time does she get up every morning?"

Said the boy: "At 4 o'clock, General."

Hideki Tojo was pleased. "It is mothers like that," he said, "who will win the War."

On occasion, Tojo also inspected prisoner-of-war camps. On one such visit he arrived at Omori, between Tokyo and Yokohama, just as British prisoners were taking their weekly baths. They were ordered to stand at attention stark-naked, then bow from the waist, Japanese-style. Tojo, dressed in a gray suit and carrying an ivory-handled walking stick, seemed amused and raised his felt hat to return the salute. He checked all of the huts and asked particularly about the food supplies. To at least one of the prisoners, he seemed "not a bad old bugger."

In short, in the effort to win the War, Tojo spared himself least of all; his office lights could be seen glowing in the predawn gloom and well into the night. From his small and spartan office, Tojo presided over the stifling structure of the wartime Japanese government, an apparatus pervasive and often repressive in its control of Japanese life.

As Prime Minister, Tojo was theoretically responsible for conducting Cabinet meetings and reporting their proposals to the Emperor for his consent or disapproval. In practice, the Cabinet was an almost impotent group, and His Majesty had no options.

The real power for making policy rested with a "liaison" group that, although it might invite others to its sessions, always included the Prime Minister, the Army and Navy chiefs of staff, the ministers of the two services (both of whom were required to be senior military officers on the active-duty list) and the Foreign Minister. The military character of this elite group was accentuated by the fact that most of its decisions were based on information prepared by *chuken shoko*—staff majors and lieutenant colonels who, by reason of their role, came to have immense influence.

Once the liaison group had made up its collective mind, it went through the ritual of petitioning the Emperor for an imperial conference—a request that was routinely granted. Before such a conclave, the Emperor was briefed on the agenda by his Lord Keeper of the Privy Seal. If Emperor Hirohito expressed concern about any of the matters to be presented, the President of the Privy Council prepared a list of questions, which was given in advance to the officials scheduled to attend the imperial conference so that they could work up their replies.

The Emperor was escorted to the conference by his chief aide-de-camp, almost always an Army general, and was enthroned on a dais. At right angles to the podium were two tables, both covered with brocade, along which sat His Majesty's senior advisers, most of them bedecked with the ribbons and medals of their military trade. After Tojo had briefly outlined the decisions already made by the liaison group, the Emperor's previously prepared questions were read and the carefully rehearsed answers were given. Through it all, the Emperor of Japan almost always sat silent.

As a means of actually formulating decisions, the process was of course useless. Not once during the entire War was a proposal by the liaison group reversed or even amended at an imperial conference. Yet the system did serve a purpose: It clothed with imperial respectability the edicts by which the ruling militarists, in their single-minded drive to place Japan on a footing of total war, swept aside such democratic institutions as the nation had managed to develop during the previous century.

Among the system's offspring was a bureaucratic giant in which Tojo and his colleagues, at least during the early months of the War, placed high hopes. It was called the Imperial Rule Assistance Association, or IRAA, and its aim —according to the *Japan Year Book,* a publication put out by the quasi-official Japan Foreign Affairs Association—was to act as "the pivotal body of the national structure to guide the nation's march toward the construction of a high-tensioned defense state."

Japan's political parties had been officially dissolved in 1940, and all political activities had been placed under the aegis of the IRAA, which also proceeded to gobble

56

up labor unions, women's groups, youth corps, farm organizations and trade associations. Moreover, said the *Year Book*, "science, arts, sports and amusements must be developed in accordance with the basic purpose" of the Imperial Rule Assistance Association. With headquarters in Tokyo and with Tojo as its president ex officio, the IRAA flooded Japan with coercive orders affecting the attitudes and daily lives of all Japanese.

On paper, the Imperial Rule Assistance Association was impressive. In practice, it was a fiasco. Top-heavy with Tokyo bureaucrats and snarled by red tape, it slowly collapsed of its own weight, and although it remained on government organization charts, it was generally bypassed as the Tojo regime sought other, more direct means of imposing wartime strictures.

Far more effective than the cumbersome IRAA was the old system of *tonarigumi,* or neighborhood associations, which had been revived in 1939 for "molding the moral life of the people and their spiritual values." To that end the government passed down through the *tonarigumi* seven precepts for daily living: "Rise early, give thanks for what you have, cooperate with the authorities, render public service, be punctual, encourage thrift and enhance physical and spiritual discipline."

By the time of Japan's entry into World War II, the *tonarigumi* numbered about 1.1 million units, each composed of 10 to 12 households, with as many as 20 neighborhood associations joined to form a block association. Each *tonarigumi* had a leader, chosen by consensus, who received orders from the Home Ministry in Tokyo and circulated them as bulletins among the group's members. In that fashion the *tonarigumi* performed an almost endless number of national and municipal chores. They collected taxes. They handed out food rations. They organized air-raid drills and fought fires. They encouraged savings deposits, implemented crime-prevention measures and acted as neighborhood social groups. And although the chores that they imposed could be an infernal nuisance to busy people, they also had their pleasant side.

Journalist Kiyoshi Togasaki, for example, looked back with some nostalgia on the days of the *tonarigumi* in his hometown of Ogikubo, west of Tokyo, a diverse community of wealthy aristocrats and less-affluent teachers, bureaucrats, carpenters, noodle-shop proprietors, laundry operators and the like. "Before the *tonarigumi*," recalled Togasaki, "most people stuck to themselves and their families. You never really knew your neighbors. But the *tonarigumi* brought a sense of mutual help. We were all thrown into the same pot, with everyone on an equal footing."

But the *tonarigumi* were also charged with a sinister mission: that of helping to "do away with individualistic thinking and living." This meant collaborating with the police to eradicate even the slightest trace of dissidence in wartime Japan. With the help of intimidated informers from the neighborhood associations, the Japanese police network became a force for repression on a monumental scale.

The power of the police was based on laws of great scope and severity. People suspected of even thinking dissident thoughts were subject to arrest and imprisonment. When released, they were placed under "protection and surveillance" by policemen operating out of 22 special stations established throughout Japan. The police were ordered by the Home Ministry to investigate "the career, environment, mental and physical condition and changes in thought of the person in question." Those under surveillance were subject to police control of their dwelling places, their personal associations and their correspondence. The whole idea, as the *Japan Year Book* approvingly noted, was "to encourage 'thought' offenders to change their minds."

A Public Peace Preservation Law, originally promulgated in 1925 and drastically amended in 1941, threatened Draconian penalties for a wide array of offenses. Leaders of "secret societies for changing the national constitution" could be put to death. A sentence of life imprisonment could be imposed on the "organizers or leaders of any group, which has not yet developed into a society, working for the overthrow of the national constitution." Long prison sentences could be meted out to members of "vicious semireligious bodies" or of "any religious body that preaches doctrines detrimental to the sound interpretation of the national constitution." Similar punishment was promised for people belonging to groups "whose aim is to propagate ideas blasphemous to the dignity of the Grand Shrines of Ise or the Imperial House."

The police supervised all Japanese publications, and the

editors of newspapers or periodicals dealing with political matters were required to post bond "as a guarantee of good faith." The law required that notice of all public meetings be given to the police ahead of time, and police were authorized to stop any speech or shut down any meeting not to their liking. The police were also allowed to inspect and supervise "inns, public baths, employment exchanges for geisha and prostitutes, credit-information businesses, barbers, seal or stamp engravers, old-clothes dealers, peddlers and stall-holders." Not least, policemen were assigned to "look after the maintenance of good public manners and morals," a duty that included seeing that "the prostitutes are treated as humanely as possible."

One of the most notorious of the police agencies was the *kenpeitai*, or military police, whose Kwantung Army branch General Tojo himself had headed in the 1930s while serving in Manchuria. In Japan as well as overseas, the *kenpei* were not satisfied merely with enforcing law and order within the military establishment; they enthusiastically turned their baneful attention to civilians as well, ostensibly in the name of national security.

Two other organizations, the *tokko*, or special higher police, and the national police, a force similar to the U.S. Federal Bureau of Investigation, also were charged with safeguarding national security—a task they carried out in much the same heavy-handed manner as their German counterpart, the Gestapo. The system was rounded out with myriad metropolitan and local police forces, and Tojo indirectly controlled it all through the Home Ministry.

Both as Prime Minister and as War Minister, Tojo had direct control over the *kenpeitai*, and he kept the massive force under standing orders to make arrests on the slightest suspicion of subversion, disloyal thought, expressions of dissidence or disrespect for the Emperor.

Although Japan almost certainly suffered less from espionage than any other nation involved in World War II, the nation's fear of spies was manic. Soldiers were moved only at night. Passengers on trains passing by the Navy bases at Yokosuka, Kure and Sasebo had to pull down the curtains on the side toward the sea so they could not see the ships in the harbors—even though the local townspeople saw them every day. When the battleship *Yamato*, at 68,000 tons the largest warship afloat (along with its sister ship, the *Musa-*

shi), was being built at Kure, the shipyard was fenced in with enough steel to construct two destroyers.

In such a climate, the *kenpeitai* thrived. The military policemen searched the luggage of passengers on trains. They detained and grilled anyone found reading an English-language book. They confiscated and examined diaries, needing only the slightest pretext to shout accusations of leftist leanings. One woman, Chizuko Matsumoto, recalled that two *kenpei* had burst into her room while she and a friend were listening to a record of *La Cumparsita*, a South American tango. "You traitors!" they cried. "The nation is in a grave emergency but you listen to enemy music!" Before leaving, they smashed most of Matsumoto's records.

Behind such seemingly casual outrages was a deliberate design. "The rumor was that if the *kenpeitai* took you away, that was the end," recalled one Japanese. "They wanted everyone quaking with fear." As early as 1942 the *kenpeitai's* calculated terror campaign had gone to such excess that murmurs of protest were heard even from the submissive citizenry; for example, an anonymous letter sent to a government office in Tokyo demanded that Japan be permitted to become "a free country like America."

The complaints prompted the *kenpeitai's* commander, Major General Hakuji Kato, to make a public defense of his force. To be sure, he said, some of the *kenpeitai's* methods may have seemed "a little too stringent." The unfortunate result was that the *kenpei* were sometimes "looked on with fear and suspicion as a kind of secret-police force." This, said Kato, was most distressing. "You need not fear them," he blandly assured his countrymen. In any case, he concluded, the measures taken by the *kenpeitai* were "inevitable to bring us final victory in the Greater East Asia War." And the *kenpeitai* went its way untrammeled.

The *tokko*, the *kenpeitai's* rival for police-state supremacy, was a force established in 1911 to suppress left-wing movements and to censor the press. Now, its franchise greatly expanded, it specialized in enforcing the thought-control provisions of the law.

Members of the *tokko* were authorized to make two kinds of arrests, one for questioning, the other for detention. Supposedly, the maximum period of detention was 29 days, after which the prisoner either was released or had charges filed against him. The *tokko* got around that bothersome requirement by holding a suspect in one station for the maximum period, then transferring him to another place of detention, where the 29-day cycle began again. Once detained, a suspect was usually thrown into a cell and forced to sit on his haunches, straight and unmoving, for as long as 24 hours at a time. Recalled one prisoner: "The sun rose, noon came, evening fell and night came, and we were not allowed to do anything but sit on the floor, our knees folded. If we tried to stretch our legs and got caught, we were kicked around."

Persons arrested for ideological or political reasons frequently were ordered to write their memoirs. The *tokko* demanded that each account cover certain specifics: family background, the circumstances under which the suspect had lived and grown up, the names of friends and associates, political and social activities, a career résumé, an essay on the prisoner's political outlook and how he had arrived at it. It was a hopeless circle: If the suspect did not write what the *tokko* wanted to see, he was forced to start over again; if he wrote what the *tokko* wished, he was charged with a political crime.

A fairly typical *tokko* arrest came one cold winter night when three *tokko* agents, all clad in black coats, arrived without warning at the residence of motion-picture director Akira Iwasaki, who was considered a liberal. Iwasaki, roused from his sleep, was taken without explanation to the Ikebukuro police station in northwest Tokyo. At the same time, his books, magazines, notebooks, diaries and manuscripts were tied in bundles and carted off to the station. (Later in the War, when fuel shortages became critical, they were burned to provide warmth for the police.) Hauled before a *tokko* official in the morning, Iwasaki was told that he was to be "chilled"—confined in an unheated cell. In all, Iwasaki remained in jail for 14 months without going to trial; ultimately he was released with a warning to refrain from all political expression or activity.

Later in the War, Yoshimi Furui, head of the *tokko's* thought-control bureau, told the Diet that he meant to stiffen national resolve with an intensified crackdown on activities "harmful to unity within the country." He was as good as his word: The *tokko* in a district near Tokyo arrested members of the editorial staffs of *Kaizo* and *Chuo Koron*, two respected magazines, and accused them of fostering Communist attitudes. A *tokko* inspector named Takeshima boldly threatened Hidetoshi Kuroda, the editor of *Chuo Koron*: "We know very well that you are not a Communist," he said. "But if you intend to be stubborn about this, we know how to handle you. We'll just set you up as a Communist. We can kill Communists." Unfazed, the journalist repeatedly said that he was unaware of any Communists or sympathizers on his staff. Kuroda was released, but his magazine was shut down for the rest of the War.

Victories won through repression at home grew ever more important as the number of Japanese victories on the battlefield and at sea declined. By June 1942, when the Imperial Combined Fleet failed to win the Battle of Midway, Japan's great adventure had begun to turn sour. To keep the news of the Midway disaster from the Japanese people, Prime Minister Tojo ordered that the survivors of ships sunk in the battle be kept in isolation. The Japanese high command unabashedly announced that the Imperial Navy had at last "secured supreme power in the Pacific"; in Tokyo, this deception sent celebrating throngs into the streets for flag processions and lantern parades.

For so long as the lightning-swift strikes of Japan's armed forces had been marked by unbroken success, Tojo and his colleagues had been content to accept public applause while allowing the Emperor to remain silent and unseen in the background. After Midway, however, they increasingly relied on imperial prestige, urging members of the Imperial Family to pay morale-boosting visits to military bases, industrial plants and schools. Beginning in early 1943, hardly a month went by without an imperial rescript—historically promulgated only on momentous occasions—being issued to exhort the home front to greater efforts and to assure the Japanese people that eventual victory was certain.

Cheapening the sacred authority of the imperial rescript was foolish. Corrupting it was far worse, but in mid-1943 Tojo did just that. Withholding the somber facts from the Emperor, he persuaded His Majesty to announce that Japan had won a "great victory" in the Solomon Islands—at a time when Japanese forces actually were withdrawing from the area in abject defeat.

As Japanese troops retreated from their conquered territories, as an American submarine blockade steadily tightened its grip on the home islands, and as the Japanese people and Japanese industry began to feel the pangs of serious shortages, Prime Minister Tojo found one occasion for satisfaction. In November 1943, cooperative representatives of China, Manchukuo (the name given by the Japanese to their Manchurian satrapy), Thailand, Burma and the Philippines gathered in Tokyo for a conference of the Greater East Asia Co-Prosperity Sphere.

Tojo was a devout believer in Pan-Asianism and, unlike many of his more cynical Japanese colleagues, he may have sincerely believed that all of the peoples of Asia would prosper under Japanese control. It was characteristic of his thinking that he had once explained the Japanese onslaught against China in terms of economic cooperation between the two nations. "The basic intention," he said, "was that the raw materials that China possessed in abundance would

be contributed by China, and the techniques, capital and skilled personnel would be contributed by Japan. The idea of mutual benefit was the main one. It had a moral basis."

Now, as chairman of the Greater East Asia Conference, Tojo sat at the head of a horseshoe-shaped table and opened the conclave upon which rested whatever remaining hopes he had that Japan might yet emerge from the War with some gain. "It is an incontrovertible fact," he said, "that the nations of Greater East Asia are bound in every respect by ties of an inseparable relationship."

One after another, Japan's puppets proclaimed their Pan-Asian aspirations. Said Wang Ching-wei, the head of Japan's client government in China: "All the nations of East Asia should love their own countries, love their neighbors and love East Asia."

José Laurel, President of the Philippines, which had recently been granted nominal independence by Japan, spoke

Japanese couples enjoy a final dance to the strains of "Auld Lang Syne" on October 31, 1940. The government had ordered all dance halls to close at the stroke of midnight that night as a conservation measure.

60

in a voice quavering with emotion: "There is no longer any power that can stop or delay the acquisition by the one billion Orientals of the free and untrammeled right and opportunity to shape their own destiny. God in His infinite wisdom will not abandon Japan and will not abandon the peoples of Greater East Asia. God will descend from Heaven, weep with us, and glorify the courage and bravery of our peoples and enable us to liberate ourselves."

Last of the orators was Cambridge-educated Dr. Ba Maw, the first Premier of Burma, which like the Philippines recently had achieved token independence. "For years in Burma I dreamed my Asian dreams," declared Ba Maw. "My Asian blood has always called to other Asians. In my dreams, both sleeping and waking, I have heard the voice of Asia calling to her children. This is not the time to think with our minds; this is the time to think with our blood."

For Tojo, the unanimous adoption by the conference of a resolution calling for cooperation and friendship among the nations of Greater East Asia was cause for enormous satisfaction. He realized that only if the peoples of East Asia joined with the Japanese in repelling the Western Allies could Japan turn back the enemy tide. Such a grass-roots alliance conceivably might have happened: The appeal of Pan-Asianism in the face of Western exploitation had enormous power. But whatever opportunity Pan-Asianism may have offered to Japan had already been demolished by the Japanese soldiers' brutal treatment of the peoples who had fallen under their control.

Tojo's efforts to put together an effective East Asian coalition had been further undermined by forces within his own government. In a document titled "Basic Concepts of the Greater East Asia Co-Prosperity Sphere," the Imperial Rule Assistance Association declared: "Though we use the expression 'Asian cooperation,' this by no means ignores the fact that Japan was created by the gods, nor posits an automatic racial equality." Speaking of the Japanese occupation of territories once held by Western powers, Tojo's Cabinet Secretary, Naoki Hoshino, insisted: "There are no restrictions on us. We can take them, do anything we want."

This attitude, springing as it did from Japan's age-old sense of superiority over its neighbors, ultimately was fatal in every East Asian land in which Japanese soldiers and administrators set foot.

In Korea, which had been annexed by Japan in 1910, discrimination by the Japanese against the Koreans had become a way of life. The average income of the Japanese was more than three times that of the Koreans. Koreans drafted into the Japanese Army were reminded of their inferior status by such remarks as, "Watch your step. Don't get the idea that you are Japanese." Koreans were obliged to parrot an oath that began: "We are subjects of the great Japanese Empire. We are loyal to His Imperial Majesty the Emperor." All Koreans were required to attend Shinto services, and Korean women were subject to conscription as "comfort girls" for Japanese troops.

In Manchuria, heavy industry, transportation and communications were completely controlled by Japanese capital, and Chinese were seized as laborers to help Japan exploit the area's natural resources. The workers, according to one witness, were required to toil "with their legs manacled. The labor was exhausting, the hours long, the treatment brutal. Many fled, some to Russia. The unlucky ones who were caught were tortured by burning and by dripping water and then strung up someplace."

In north and central China, Japanese soldiers committed frightful atrocities—of which the Rape of Nanking in 1937 was only the most notorious example. A Japanese corporal returning from central China in 1942 boasted to friends: "While out foraging for supplies we got hold of a pregnant woman. We stuck our bayonets in her huge belly and skewered her like a piece of meat." One Japanese soldier told of seeing others "beat a Chinese with rocks until his skull split open and he fell in a pool of blood. Then they kicked him and threw more stones. Officers watched the killing and did nothing." In many combat sectors, Japanese policy was to put the torch to everything along its Army's line of march. Recalled a soldier: "Every village and hamlet in the operations zone was burned to the ground. Not even a single puppy was left alive."

In Malaya, about 70,000 transplanted Chinese were arrested after the fall of Singapore early in 1942. Several thousand of them, found guilty of subversive activities, were tied in groups, loaded onto boats, taken out to sea and shoved overboard. Singapore's famed Raffles Hotel was placed out of bounds to the city's residents, and leading theaters were open to Japanese only. Some schools were taken over by the Japanese for use as Army barracks and others were converted into brothels.

In Burma, the Dutch East Indies, French Indochina and the American Philippines, the Japanese were hailed at first as liberators from Western colonialism—but the welcome soon turned to dismay, then to hatred and widespread guerrilla resistance. Typically, in the Philippine countryside mass beheadings were not uncommon. More than one entire barrio was exterminated by the Japanese, its inhabitants bayoneted and its buildings burned. In Manila, the capital, Filipinos who refused to bow three times to Japanese soldiers were strung up in the city square and their bodies left to swing as grim reminders of their offense. Those found guilty of more serious crimes, such as striking a Japanese soldier, were chained to sheets of galvanized iron and fried alive in the tropical sun.

Such wanton and feckless cruelties were of course fatal to a meaningful Greater East Asia Co-Prosperity Sphere—and damaging to Japan itself. The Japanese were deprived of a bottomless reservoir of manpower for both military and civilian pursuits, and because of the inherent inefficiencies of a system based on coercion rather than cooperation, they also lost the full use of the vast natural resources that Japan so terribly needed.

Yet for all the harm it did to Japan's war effort, the failure of the Greater East Asia Co-Prosperity Sphere paled in comparison with the deleterious effects of a fierce, war-long competition between the Japanese Army and Navy, which brought disaster after disaster not only to field operations but to the nation's entire effort to mobilize its economy.

While conferring the position of Prime Minister upon Tojo in 1941, the Emperor of Japan had addressed himself—as usual, somewhat obliquely—to a problem that had long afflicted his Empire's armed forces. Said Hirohito: "Bear in mind, at this time, that cooperation between the Army and the Navy should be closer than ever before. It is Our intention to summon the Navy Minister also and to speak to him in this same vein."

Never was an admonishment so solidly founded—or so consistently ignored. Rivalries, often bitter, have existed throughout history between the armies and navies of nearly every nation. But the mutual hatred of the Japanese services was virtually without parallel. It reached deep into the past, back to bloody feudal warfare between clans. When the modern Japanese Army and Navy were founded during the Meiji Restoration in the latter 19th Century, some clans sent their sons into one service while their age-old rivals provided men to the other. The hostility between them persisted, even in the face of common enemies.

The interservice war was waged at a personal level. Admiral Isoroku Yamamoto, who engineered both the bold attack on Pearl Harbor and the subsequent loss at Midway, once showed his disdain for the Army by pulling the chair out from under a long-winded general. Admiral Soemu Toyoda, a wartime commander in chief of the Combined Fleet, often referred to the Army as "horse dung" and repeatedly declared that he would rather have his daughter marry a beggar than an Army man. But that was nothing compared with the ruinous impact of Army-Navy rivalry on economic mobilization, on the procurement and allocation of strategic supplies, on military design and manufacturing and on the distribution of finished products.

On paper, supplies for the Army and Navy were apportioned and regulated by the Ministry of Commerce and Industry, which shared the responsibility for formulating economic policy with a Cabinet Planning Board. The two services, however, refused to make available to the civilian agencies (or to each other) any data concerning their receipts and inventories of strategic materials, thereby making realistic planning impossible.

Early in the War an attempt was made to remedy the situation by granting considerable power to so-called control associations, which were given official status as government agencies; each association was headed by a civilian leader from a particular industry involved in the war effort. The Army and the Navy responded by ignoring the control associations, continuing to use their stockpiled raw materials at will and placing orders directly with manufacturing firms (some of which were owned by the services). Chaos ensued.

Interservice quarreling was at its worst in the crucial aircraft industry, in which each military branch formed and operated its own control association. Ginjiro Fujihara, a civilian economic planner who surveyed the aircraft industry, later complained: "The Navy was ahead of the Army in technical skills and the Army tried its best to catch up. Then the Navy tried to keep ahead of the Army and so the thing developed into an intense struggle for supremacy."

By the summer of 1943, Fujihara's study showed that although Japan had the plant capacity to build 53,000 airplanes per year, it was in fact producing fewer than 10,000. He explained: "The Army and Navy were stirring up a lot of fuss with their competition but they were not producing many results. They had very large factories and pretty good machinery, but when the Army built a big plant, the Navy built one too. There was a lot of competition but little thought of efficiency." One result of such wasteful operations was that only 55 per cent of the precious aluminum allocated to aircraft manufacturing actually went into airplanes; the rest ended up as scrap on the black market.

The Army and Navy raced headlong to see which could outdo the other in the field of aircraft design. By the end of

Correspondent Takeo Shinmyo enraged Tojo by siding with the Navy in a strategy dispute.

Shinmyo (first row, far left) poses with his squadron, which was later wiped out defending Iwo Jima.

A STORY THAT BROUGHT A "SUMMONS TO DEATH"

On the 23rd of February, 1944, the Japanese newspaper *Mainichi Shimbun* published a front-page article so infuriating to Prime Minister Tojo that he tried to ensure the death of its author, a war correspondent named Takeo Shinmyo.

Titled "Bamboo Spears Will Not Do the Job," Shinmyo's story criticized the Army's defense plan, which enjoined every man, woman and child on the home islands to repulse an Allied invasion with any weapon at hand. Shinmyo argued the Navy's point of view instead: The final battle would have to be fought at sea to keep the Americans from capturing island bases from which they could bomb Japan.

Although the article did not mention Tojo by name, the Prime Minister considered it a personal affront. He issued what was called a "summons-to-death" draft notice for Shinmyo a fortyish man who normally would not have been conscripted. Anyone receiving this kind of notice was shipped off to almost certain death with a frontline unit—in Shinmyo's case, an Army Air Force squadron on Iwo Jima.

But the Navy came to the journalist's rescue. It sent him its own draft notice, which carefully predated the Army's, and snatched him away to a safer job in the Navy Press Corps.

the War, the Navy had produced 53 basic aircraft models that had 112 variations; the Army had 37 basic models with 52 variations. Many of these planes were copies of foreign models that had fallen into Japanese hands.

The feuding went to equally absurd lengths in the matter of procuring oil from the conquered Dutch East Indies. The Navy, which needed oil desperately, had to get much of it from those islands. The Army, preponderantly an infantry force, needed fuel for its air corps and little else. Yet the Army had virtually monopolized Japan's oil sources.

This imbalance arose from a peculiar arrangement: Oil stocks in the captured territories were divided according to which service was primarily responsible for seizing a particular place. In this, the Army had a distinct advantage: Its holding of major production fields and six huge refineries gave it 85 per cent of the oil resources in the former Dutch islands, leaving the Navy little more than what it could get out of two ports in Borneo.

To satisfy its far greater need for oil, the Navy had to resort to extortion, threatening to withhold the tankers that carried oil to Japan unless the Army parted with more oil. The disputes worsened, in spite of the formation of an Army-Navy oil committee to resolve differences. The committee's directives to service representatives in the field were usually ignored.

In the meantime, the Navy's chronic oil shortage contributed frequently and dramatically to the losing of the war at sea. During the great carrier-based air battle off the Mariana Islands in June of 1944, a Japanese fleet was in the vicinity but could not enter the fighting because its warships were low on fuel. Left free from attack by surface ships, the American carriers launched and retrieved their planes at will in the "Turkey Shoot" from which Japanese air power never recovered. Later, in the Battle for Leyte Gulf, the battleships *Ise* and *Hyuga,* which had been rushed from the home islands to take part, arrived too late to be of help because they had been conserving fuel.

Although the Navy held a monopoly on tankers, the Army built its own shipyards and was very much in the business of merchant shipping; in fact, at the start of the War the Army controlled vessels whose total weight amounted to 2.1 million tons, compared with 1.7 million tons for the civilian Shipping Control Association and only 1.5 million tons for the Imperial Japanese Navy. Operationally, the two services made no effort to cooperate: Neither the Army, from its shipping headquarters at Ujina, nor the Navy, from its transportation office at Yokosuka, ever exchanged information about shipping departures, routes, cargoes, arrivals—or even the sightings of enemy submarines.

The Army, not content with operating its own merchant fleet, even used its dominant political position to muscle into the construction of submarines. Recalled Vice Admiral Shigeyoshi Miwa, commander of the Navy's submarine fleet: "When the Army proposed to build its own submarines, the Navy opposed the plan. But the Army answered that it was planning special submarines for supplying the islands, and it didn't want to use Navy submarines for such work because Navy submarines had more important missions to fight with the fleet. The Navy agreed with that. The Navy also explained to the Army that the building of submarines was very difficult, and said it wanted to show the Army how to build them. But the Army did not want the Navy's help, and built the submarines itself." Not surprisingly, the Army submarines were of little use.

Japan's failure to develop an efficient radar during the War also can be blamed in part on the interservice rivalry. American radar experts, in a postwar report, declared that "very severe criticism must be leveled at those Japanese military leaders who so long insisted that Army and Navy research, development, production and operation be kept entirely separated. The number of scientists in Japan sufficiently skilled to undertake radar research was inadequate to begin with. It was then the height of folly to insist on reducing their effectiveness by nearly one half by requiring all projects, ofttimes parallel, to be studied secretly within each of the two services."

The Army had supreme authority for military conscription, and it had no compunction whatever about drafting skilled aircraft workers into its own uniformed rank and file, especially when the men were employed at plants producing primarily for the Navy. At one point it was estimated that about 4,500 workers, or 50 per cent of the entire work force of the Kyushu Airplane Company, had been conscripted. They were replaced by inexperienced and unskilled women, students and Koreans. And the two services seemed to take pleasure in ordering their suppliers to produce different items to serve the same purpose. "Even in such a matter as ordering a screw," recalled Masuo Kato, a journalist for Japan's Domei News Agency, "the Army might specify a left-handed screw, while the Navy demanded a right-handed thread on an otherwise identical item."

By November 1943, Japanese industry was in such a confused state that the Cabinet Planning Board and the Ministry of Commerce and Industry were both abolished. Replacing them, with the specific assignment to clean up the mess created by the opposing services, was a brand-new Munitions Ministry—with Hideki Tojo at its head.

Private firms involved in war production of any kind were designated "munitions companies," a dubious honor that was eventually bestowed upon 671 manufacturers. The Munitions Ministry was given sole power to regulate the companies' production schedules. The ministry also controlled the funds of the subjugated firms, and could merge them or dissolve them as it saw fit.

The Munitions Ministry failed ingloriously—a fact neatly documented by the rapid changeover at the head of the ministry. Tojo was soon so disgusted with the job that he turned it over to Nobusuke Kishi, his vice minister. Kishi was succeeded by economist Ginjiro Fujihara, a tough and efficient former executive of the Mitsui industrial complex. Fujihara resigned in exasperation and was replaced by a bureaucratic muddler named Yoshida. Explained Fujihara: "The question was to get somebody acceptable to both the Army and the Navy, and so they agreed on a compromise man—Yoshida—who could not do anything anyway. Perhaps they thought that by having a man who didn't know anything, they could both have their way."

Throughout the War years, it was evident that the two services needed—and would never accept—a joint command. Shortly after the Battle of Midway, Rear Admiral So-

kichi Takagi dared to suggest to the Navy General Staff that Japan's only hope for success lay in the unification of Army and Navy activities under a Supreme Command. But both services resisted practical cooperation, even in battle zones.

Authority in combat areas was assigned to one service or the other for no evident reason. The Army got most such commands, but the Navy received half of New Guinea, the Solomon Islands, the Celebes and the mandated Marshall, Caroline and Mariana Islands. Neither service felt any responsibility for a territory within the other's jurisdiction—a fact to which journalist Kato, for one, attributed the loss of Saipan in June 1944. "Japanese marines," wrote Kato, "were insufficient in number to defend the area assigned to the Navy, and the support given by the Army was inadequate and half-hearted."

The Navy was no more supportive. As the Army's part of Admiral Yamamoto's Midway operation, Japanese soldiers had seized and fortified the Aleutian Island of Attu. The Navy had opposed the landing and was quick to criticize it. "We should have just pounded Attu and withdrawn from there," Vice Admiral Takijiro Onishi said later. "But we took a foolish liking to the place and poured in too much matériel and unnecessary personnel, making it impossible to leave." The "unnecessary personnel" were some 2,300 soldiers who were stranded there when the United States recaptured Attu in May 1943.

Emperor Hirohito was deeply disturbed when he learned of the fiasco at Attu. In full innocence, he asked his aide-de-camp, "Are the Navy and the Army really frank with each other? If there is friction between them, this war cannot be concluded successfully."

The Emperor was dead right in his conclusion. With Tojo engaged in a futile struggle to master Japan's sprawling administrative structure, with the oppressive hand of the police felt in every corner of the land and with the Army and the Navy at constant odds, the outmanned and outgunned Japanese Empire was moving inexorably down the road to defeat. The Japanese people, still steadfast in spirit even as they entered into a period of nightmare, would suffer the consequences.

THE GOSPEL OF PATRIOTISM

Showing their contempt for the United States, pedestrians in Tokyo walk across a huge American flag painted on the sidewalk by government propagandists.

BODIES AND SOULS PRIMED FOR ALL-OUT WAR

"We were reminded of the soldiers fighting for our country in northern China," said a Japanese schoolgirl, explaining why she and her classmates had gone coatless one winter. That the children suffered the cold without complaining was a tribute to their patriotism and to the Japanese government's efforts at what it called spiritual mobilization—a relentless propaganda campaign that was designed to put the nation in step with the military and to steel all segments of the population to the hardships that war would bring to the home front.

Tokyo's propaganda machine went into high gear the day after Pearl Harbor, when the nation's newspapers were ordered to prepare all news "in cooperation with the government." Thereafter, the Japanese people were deluged with headlines and stories proclaiming the bravery of Japan's selfless soldiers and the righteousness of its holy war to defend the Emperor against the fiendish American aggressors.

Any citizen who questioned the government line might find himself interrogated or even imprisoned by an organization called, with startling candor, the Thought Police. When the cowed, cooperative press slipped on occasion and printed comments that violated a 1941 law against fomenting "peace sentiment," the offending writers faced the loss of their jobs or a term in jail. Many newspapers prepared for such mistakes by employing "jail editors" whose sole function was to serve the required time in prison.

Such measures helped to keep the press in line and to strait-jacket the people's minds. The government also attempted to regiment their bodies: Young men were required—above and beyond their daily jobs—to "volunteer" for work details; young women were exhorted to marry and to produce children to populate the expanding Empire. Both sexes of all ages were harassed into wearing drab civilian uniforms and participating in paramilitary drills. The people were told what to eat, when to exercise and how to pray, as the government strove for and, for the most part, succeeded in reaching its proclaimed goal of "flawless public order."

A militiaman rams a bamboo spear into a straw effigy of Britain's Winston Churchill. The adjacent placard urges passersby to stop and take a stab.

Japanese troops charge into battle across the huge billboard of a Tokyo theater in 1943. The advertisement bears the slogan, "We Won't Stop Shooting!"

A Tokyo police detective in a Western-style suit and straw hat scolds two women for wearing a dress and a kimono, garments that the government considered extravagant.

A woman wearing the sash of an air-raid warden cheerfully models a pair of the loose-fitting trousers, or monpe, that most of the Japanese women eventually adopted.

AUSTERITY MEASURES TO TOUGHEN THE HOMELAND

Early in the War, as the Japanese leaders planned military operations that would make huge cutbacks in consumer goods inevitable, the government launched an austerity program that was designed to prepare the civilian population for the sacrifices to come. The program's slogans—such as "Extravagance Is the Enemy"—were proclaimed on posters distributed all across the home islands.

Most Japanese complied with the government's demands. They hardened their bodies with exercise sessions led by daily broadcasts on the state-run radio network. And they tightened their belts with voluntary diet restrictions like those already practiced by the nation's Zen monks, who had vowed to forgo rice for a sparse regimen of fruits and vegetables.

People learned to live without customary conveniences. Beginning in 1940, gasoline was strictly rationed and Tokyo was closed to traffic between midnight and five in the morning. Patriotic women's groups were assigned by the authorities to report the name of any citizen caught wasting fuel by driving to the red-light district.

The government also called for sartorial restraint. Women were urged to shelve Western-style dresses and elaborate kimonos for the blouses and baggy work pants worn by farm women. Lipstick, rouge and eye make-up were banned; short, severe haircuts became the fashion as hairdressing salons closed.

Japanese men—civilians and conscripts alike—were exhorted to exchange their Western business suits for ill-fitting khaki uniforms with puttees and Army caps. Eventually, as all available leather was appropriated for making boots for the military, civilians everywhere were reduced to wearing the clumsy wooden clogs of the countryside.

70

With Mount Fuji in the background, a group of residents of the Izu Peninsula, near Tokyo, perform calisthenics in the open air.

A man and his son eat Rising Sun lunches, so called because of their resemblance to the Japanese national flag. The meal consisted of a pickled red plum set in a field of white rice.

Beaming mothers hoist a row of chubby infants in one of many healthy-baby contests held nationwide to promote motherhood.

Prospective wives of soldiers stationed in Manchuria march with hoes at a brides' school.

Teen-age workers strain to move a carload of limestone, used for making cement, at a rural branch of the Showa Electric Company.

SPECIAL CONTRIBUTIONS BY WOMEN AND CHILDREN

As the War drained Japan's manpower, those who remained at home were exhorted to make greater contributions to the nation. Children were assigned to gather charcoal and perform other simple tasks. Older students were expected to toil in the fields or factories. And young women were urged to step up production of a very special commodity—offspring.

Japan had long suffered from overpopulation and had used that fact to justify expansion. Now the government claimed it needed people to colonize its new possessions, and mounted a propaganda drive to produce three million births annually—half again as many as in peacetime.

As part of the campaign, the government banned all forms of birth control and set up matchmaking agencies and schools for brides, who were trained as colonists to wed Japanese soldiers serving overseas. The state paid for the weddings and promised free higher education for families that produced 10 or more children.

Women were encouraged "to recognize motherhood as the national destiny," and Mrs. Katsuko Tojo, wife of the Prime Minister and mother of seven, told the nation that "having babies is fun."

AN OUTPOURING OF SUNDRY SOLDIERS

The startlingly swift victories achieved by the Japanese armed forces early in the War spread a new wave of militaristic ardor throughout the nation. To urge it on, propagandists constantly reminded the Japanese people that their troops embodied the heroic virtues of the ancient samurai.

Military fever infected all strata of society. Proud mothers dressed their tots in ornate uniforms and teachers told their classes that any boy who did not serve in the "holy" war would be "shamed for life." Youngsters were further inspired by the well-publicized conscription of their heroes, Japan's professional athletes.

Even Buddhist monks, whose religion preaches nonviolence, answered the call to join up. And so many Shinto priests enlisted that, for the first time in that religion's long history, women were ordained to take the men's places.

Little boys dressed as generals and admirals gravely salute during a national children's holiday.

A rank of tall, big-bellied sumo wrestlers, the popular traditional athletes of Japan, stand at dress right during a home-guard training exercise in 1942.

With bayonets belted to their robes and rifles over their shoulders, Buddhist priests are drilled by a regular Army officer on the grounds of their temple.

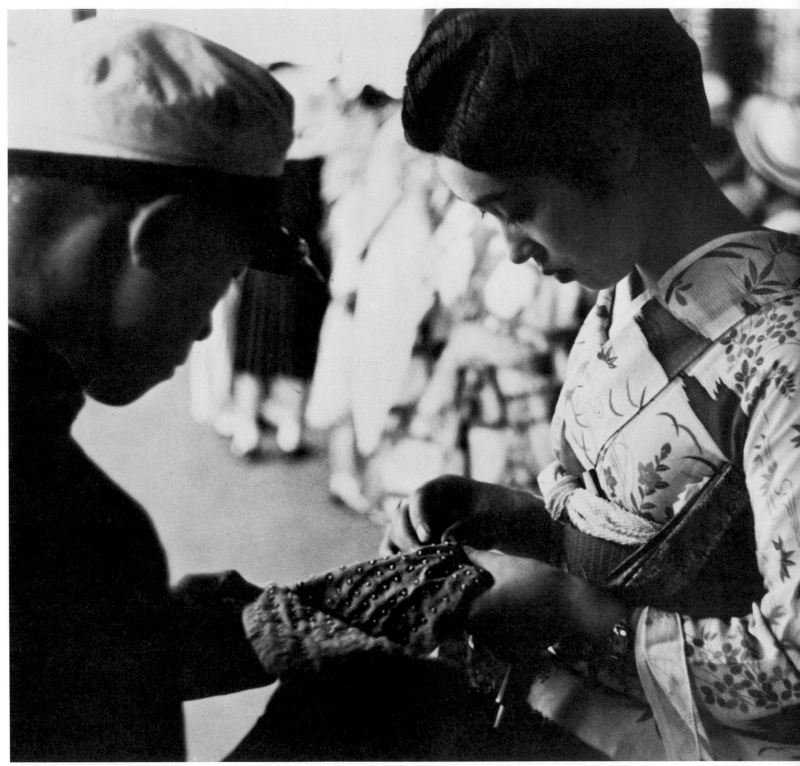

A pretty pedestrian stops on a Tokyo street in 1943 to sew a red stitch on a band of cotton cloth. After 1,000 people had completed one stitch apiece, the good-luck cloth was forwarded to a soldier at the front.

A passerby paints the Japanese character for "power" on a Rising Sun flag held by a young woman. When 1,000 characters had been inscribed, the flag was sent to a fighting man.

SYMBOLIC SUPPORT FOR THE FIGHTING MEN

The women of Japan shouldered the job of maintaining morale both at home and among the troops overseas. The National Defense Women's Organization coordinated such activities, dispatching its members to railway stations to see troops off to the fighting fronts and urging them to write letters of encouragement to servicemen. Women also sought help from total strangers in creating symbolic tokens—amulets aimed at reassuring the men that they had the wholehearted support of the nation they had left behind them.

A favorite token was the "thousand-stitch band," a piece of cloth decorated one stitch at a time by people in the streets and sent to fighting men as "a symbol of Japanese women's trust and faith." One was sent to Saburo Sakai, a leading fighter pilot, by his fiancée and his cousin. "Few Japanese airmen had faith in this traditional talisman against enemy bullets," Sakai wrote. But he thought of the hours his fiancée and cousin had "stood on the streets in the cold air of winter" to solicit decorative stitches from passersby. "Of course I would wear it," he concluded, "and I wrapped it around my midsection."

Volunteers also stood on the streets with another token, a Japanese flag on which they asked pedestrians to inscribe good-luck wishes. Many a soldier went into battle carrying a signed flag—the revered symbol of his nation—in his pocket.

PRAYERS AT A SACRED SHRINE FOR THE DEAD

The Japanese were encouraged to pray publicly at Tokyo's huge, somber Yasukuni Shrine, where the souls of all slain soldiers were believed to reside. This belief was buttressed early in the War by Emperor Hirohito. Presiding at a solemn Shinto rite at Yasukuni, he enshrined the souls of the 10,334 officers already killed in China, thus making them *kami,* or immortals, almost on a level with himself.

As the number of war dead mounted inexorably, thousands of bereaved citizens prayed at the shrine each day. So sacred was the site that passing streetcars would pause before its gates while the passengers stood and bowed.

Mourners kneel in the rain outside Yasukuni Shrine in downtown Tokyo in 1941. Civilians regularly

made the popular pilgrimage to pray for their loved ones lost in war. Many soldiers also prayed there before shipping out to one of the fighting fronts.

THE IMPERIAL CAPTIVE

Visiting Great Britain in 1921, Crown Prince Hirohito salutes an honor guard. His escort, in bearskin hat, is the Prince of Wales, later King Edward VIII.

A SHY, PEACE-LOVING, OBEDIENT EMPEROR

"Sublime is the moment," wrote Emperor Hirohito in one of his brief, fragile poems, "when the world is at peace." Yet such was his training within the ironbound Japanese tradition that this peace-loving man rarely spoke out for peace.

Born in 1901, Hirohito grew up in a loveless atmosphere that stifled and cowed him. As court custom dictated, he was taken from his parents at the age of 10 weeks and placed in the hands of a succession of guardians and tutors; for a time, 11 scholars drummed as many subjects into the boy's head.

In spite of this regimen, the Crown Prince showed signs of intellectual independence. At the age of 12 he shocked his history teacher by disputing the myth that he was a descendant of the sun goddess and therefore a god himself. His chief guardian, Prince Saionji, warned him against uttering such heresies and explained that the Japanese people needed to believe that their Emperor was sacred. For the good of the nation, Saionji said, Hirohito must maintain a godlike dignity and remoteness, and never involve himself in the affairs of the world.

Hirohito grew into a shy, self-effacing man, though he somehow maintained a modicum of personal freedom. He became a serious scientist, indulged in Western sports and even dared to defy the powerful advisers who objected to a marriage that he favored. But in all matters concerning his imperial role, he remained a rigid conformist to the laws and conventions that had long since reduced the Emperor to a priestly figurehead. He was unworldly and excessively trusting.

As Japan's military clique drove the nation toward war with China and later with the Western Allies, Hirohito never made a forceful appeal to deflect the aggressive leaders from their course. Instead he obliquely spoke of his concern in a poem he composed: "As I was visiting Cape Shio in Kii / Clouds were hanging low far over the Sea." Although the Emperor seemed not to realize it, his moral authority was immense, and in failing to use it he contributed to Japan's wartime tragedy.

Hirohito's parents, Emperor Taisho and Empress Teimei, relinquished the Crown Prince's upbringing to guardians in accordance with court custom.

Hirohito, shown here as a three-year-old, lived apart from his parents in a small building in the palace compound staffed by more than 3,000 servants.

Dressed in tennis whites, Hirohito and his wife, Nagako, team up for a game of doubles in 1924, three years after his return from Europe.

Saluting bystanders, Hirohito rides through London with King George V at the beginning of his eye-opening, 20-day British visit.

Empress Nagako cradles tiny Crown Prince Akihito in a portrait with the Emperor—in a Western business suit—and their daughters.

Hirohito pauses momentarily in his study of marine biology in his palace laboratory. He later published scholarly works on the subject.

AN EASTERN PRINCE'S WESTERN WAYS

The happiest period of his life, Hirohito once confessed, was his six-month grand tour of Europe in 1921. "I experienced for the first time," he fondly recalled, "what it was to live more freely."

The 20-year-old Crown Prince was astounded by the relative informality of the British Royal Family. He was delighted to find that his counterpart, the Prince of Wales, was permitted to dine in public restaurants and dance with pretty girls in nightclubs. He idolized bluff King George V, who once gave him a fatherly slap on the back and called him "Me boy."

Hirohito returned to Japan with a number of Western interests. He played tennis and had a nine-hole golf course built inside the Imperial Palace grounds. He switched to eating an English breakfast of eggs and toast (rather than rice) and began wearing Western clothes except on most ceremonial occasions. He even wore a Western felt hat during the annual rice-shoot planting ceremony, while all his officials wore the rice planter's traditional broad-brimmed straw hat.

He chose to be a Western-style husband—monogamous despite the considerable risk to the succession. After Hirohito became Emperor, he and his wife, Nagako, produced only daughters, who could not inherit the throne. Hirohito resisted intense pressure from his advisers to accept the immemorial solution of taking concubines until one of them bore him a son and heir to the throne. Hirohito's fidelity was rewarded when Nagako, in 1933, gave birth to a son at last.

Wearing traditional ceremonial robes and holding a scepter, Emperor Hirohito is formally enthroned in the ancient Imperial Palace in Kyoto, in 1928.

Suspecting an attempt on Hirohito's life, troops in front of the Emperor's limousine grab a soldier who actually intended to complain of Army mistreatment.

Squatting villagers were still permitted to view the Emperor in 1930.

Osaka's mayor was forced to resign for standing casually with Hirohito.

STORM CENTER IN A CLASH OF CULTURES

Through the late 1920s and most of the 1930s, Hirohito was caught between conflicting ideals and ambitions. Like many other progressive young Japanese, he was convinced that the country should seek prosperity through the peaceful pursuit of Western scientific knowledge and industrial technology. However, this outlook was bitterly opposed by radical Army and Navy officers, who sought to conquer all Asia and to eliminate those in favor of peaceful progress.

Two firebrands made abortive attempts to assassinate Hirohito, and six more attempted to petition him to improve conditions in Japan. Several moderate politicians were murdered by jingoists and right-wing military officers; among the victims was Prime Minister Takashi Hara, who had been accused of encouraging Hirohito's 1921 European trip.

The chiefs of the Japanese Army protested that they could not control their homicidal junior officers, but some of the Army chiefs secretly approved the violence and benefited from it. The ever-present threat of assassination intimidated some of Hirohito's liberal Cabinet members and advisers, and they in turn counseled the Emperor to remain above the growing turmoil by playing his traditional role: distant, untouchable, awe-inspiring.

This was precisely what the Army brass wanted: an Emperor who was immured within the palace grounds and unable to interfere with their plans for conquest, but also a deity who would unite and inspire the nation when war came.

The military introduced a propaganda campaign that alienated Hirohito further. Ordinary people, once allowed to view their Emperor, were now required to bow low in his presence and refrain from looking upon so exalted a personage. Certain high officials were permitted to look with respect at Hirohito, but some were hounded from office for allegedly failing to pay him sufficient homage.

A Foreign Office representative named Toshikazu Kase saw through the Army's tactics, declaring that the war-loving generals had "deliberately fostered the religious mythology surrounding the imperial dynasty." The Emperor, Kase added poetically, "was merely the reflection of the moon in the water," whereas the "real moon was the military, which exercised the power and enjoyed all its benefits."

Hirohito himself saw that he was being revered into impotence. The Army, he said in quiet despair, was "using silk floss to suffocate me."

Subjects abase themselves before the Emperor's Tokyo palace. After 1936 the police arrested any ordinary citizen who dared to look at the Emperor.

Seated before a gold screen, Hirohito presides at a meeting of the War Council. The attending officers sit rigidly at attention with their hands on their knees.

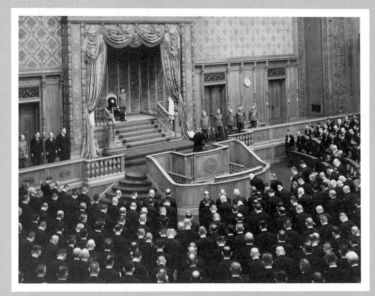

Frock-coated members of the Diet bow in unison to the Emperor (rear).

Hirohito watches troops stage an amphibious landing during maneuvers.

FORMAL DUTIES OF A FRUSTRATED FIGUREHEAD

Law and custom denied Hirohito any real power, but demanded that he perform a wearying round of ceremonial functions. The Emperor presided at every opening of the Diet, convened formal meetings of the War Council, visited Shinto shrines on holidays, observed Army maneuvers and dressed in full military regalia (*opposite*)

to welcome foreign dignitaries to Japan.

At such meetings, critics noted, Hirohito might have exerted his moral authority, indicating his wishes more strongly and directly. He did, in fact, speak up on occasion in attempts to divert the military leaders from their warlike course. As early as the 1931 invasion of Manchuria, Hirohito urged his Cabinet to follow a "policy of nonexpansion." But, said the Imperial Chamberlain, Hirohito's effort was as useless as "driving a nail into sand."

Hirohito also spoke out for peace during the fateful Cabinet meeting of September 6, 1941, when the decision for war was made. He quoted a poem written by his grandfather, Emperor Meiji, that asked: "Why do the winds and waves of strife disrupt peace?" The Cabinet members were reportedly "awed" by Hirohito's words, but the military leaders were also "relieved" that the Emperor had spoken allusively rather than directly. The generals went right ahead with their plans for war.

Waiting to greet the Emperor of Manchuria in 1935, Hirohito banters with an off-camera relative. The picture was banned—the Emperor looked too human.

From behind the palace moat, Hirohito watches a crowd hail the fall of Singapore in February 1942.

RARE OUTINGS FOR THE SON OF HEAVEN

After the attack on Pearl Harbor, Hirohito became a virtual prisoner in his palace. He emerged only rarely—to celebrate a great Japanese victory *(above)* and later, when the tide of war turned against Japan, to inspect bomb-ravaged Tokyo *(opposite)*. In 1945 he spent much of his time confined in the palace bomb shelter.

The Emperor made the most poignant sacrifice he could to the war effort: He renounced his beloved study of marine biology as a self-indulgence inappropriate in wartime. Instead he penned messages of encouragement and commendation to his fighting forces and prayed for them. The sufferings of his people so distressed him that, after the summer of 1942, Cabinet members and palace officials conspired to keep the worst news from him. He hoped for a quick end to the conflict—even as his military chiefs urged the Japanese to greater valor and bloodshed in his name.

Booted and in uniform, Hirohito walks ahead of his retinue through a bombed-out section of Tokyo in March 1945, after the worst air raid of the War.

3

The War came home to Japan in the summer of 1943. From then on the Japanese people lived and worked under ever greater stress as more and more resources were drained out of the civilian economy to support the armed forces. By the autumn of 1944, even before the heavy American bombing began, the Japanese had slid deep into what they would call the Valley of Darkness.

In strategic terms, the events of this period merely confirmed a secret prewar study whose conclusion was later summed up by one of its authors, economist Hidezo Inaba: "We came to understand that if Japan went to war, our lives would be destroyed. Not only the Japanese economy but the nation itself would succumb in great pain and desperation." Ignoring this and every other warning, the Japanese government had tried to win a short war in 1942; failing in that, Japan could not match the enormous American build-up of war production and military manpower. By 1943 an Allied naval blockade, chiefly composed of U.S. submarines, was steadily cutting down the big merchant fleet on which Japan depended for much of its food and nearly all of its vital raw materials.

The Japanese people felt the War as those in every belligerent nation did—in shortages, rationing, inflation, the black market, longer hours of harder work. But their hardships in the Valley of Darkness had a special bitterness. Despite the government's ironhanded suppression of the news of Japanese defeats, the people had a growing sense that the War was lost, and increasingly they moved like robots through their grinding days of joyless duty.

In the flush of marvelous victories in 1942, the Japanese government had let war production slip. But all of that was changed by the defeats of 1943. Higher quotas were set for the war plants. The neighborhood associations, in charge of rationing at the local level, were kept busy transporting perishable food to member families and sending members to draw staples at the nearest distribution center.

Signs of austerity increased in almost every aspect of daily life. Most of the clothes still manufactured in Japan were made from a fragile cloth called *sufu* that consisted of tiny amounts of cotton woven with wood pulp and tree bark. Japan's textile industry, formerly the third largest in the world, had turned to the ersatz cloth when the War cut off its im-

IN THE VALLEY OF DARKNESS

ports of wool from Australia and cotton from India, the United States, Egypt and Brazil. Initially, the mills had tried to substitute cotton from Japanese-occupied China, but the short fibers of the northern Chinese cotton proved impossible to weave on machines designed for the longer Indian and American varieties. Eventually, the government broke up more than eight million spindles and 250,000 looms for scrap and ordered the remaining plants to keep increasing the percentage of *sufu* in cotton cloth, and to stretch wool supplies by adding rags, mulberry bark and goat hair.

Japan was entirely self-sufficient in only one textile: silk. Previously, almost all silk cloth had been exported to the West. The loss of overseas markets now provided an unexpected bonus for the home front. Japanese women discovered that silk underwear—an unheard-of luxury before the War—was not only readily available, but selling at bargain prices.

There was no such windfall when it came to footwear. The military's growing demand for boots and for aircraft and truck tires had all but halted the production of leather shoes and the rubber-soled slippers worn by most Japanese. Instead, the government stepped up the manufacture of clumsy wooden clogs and promoted them to skeptical civilians as "patriotic footwear." To help with the campaign, Dr. Kenji Takagi of Tokyo Imperial University pronounced that wearing clogs was excellent exercise in that it "enormously strengthens the little muscles at the tips of the toes." Whether or not they believed the doctor, most civilians wore the clogs and saved their last pair of prewar shoes for special occasions.

But the basic problem for everyone was to get enough to eat. Though wartime Japan escaped mass starvation, millions of civilians began experiencing pangs of unrequited hunger in 1943, and by 1944, the search for food had become a national obsession. The people spent so much time waiting in ration lines and foraging in the countryside that they seriously reduced the nation's war production.

When the war against the United States began in 1941, Japan's farmers were producing nearly 80 per cent of the rice that was the basis of every Japanese meal. The government anticipated no major problems in maintaining adequate supplies; Japanese farmers, after all, obtained one of the highest rice yields per acre in the world. The remaining

20 per cent of Japan's annual consumption was supplied by its colonies in Korea and Taiwan. The two other essential ingredients in the Japanese diet, soy sauce and bean curd, were made from soybeans imported from Manchuria.

Soon, however, the ships that normally carried rice and soybeans were being used to transport troops and ammunition. The young men whose strong backs were needed to toil on the farms were drafted into military service. The chemicals that previously had been used to fertilize the rice paddies were now being used to manufacture high explosives. And the land available for food production shrank by 8.5 per cent as the government expropriated farms as sites for war plants and air bases.

Food imports declined in 1943, and government authorities tried to stretch the rice supply by mixing it with wheat and barley. Even potatoes were being added to bring the basic ration up to the specified weight. Housewives experimented with new recipes to make the adulterated rice mixture more palatable. But their experiments were not always successful. A dish called *nukapan,* made of fried wheat flour and rice bran, was revolting to some. "It looks like good custard," wrote a disappointed woman, "but it tastes bitter, smells like horse dung and makes you cry when you eat it."

Before long, even upright citizens were hatching shady schemes to obtain extra rations. When pregnant women were granted a daily supplement of 70 grams of rice, there was a suspicious increase in the number of expectant mothers. Gwen Terasaki, the American wife of a Japanese diplomat who spent the War years in Japan, recalled seeing one woman go to the head of a ration line to pick up her special allocation. But as the woman was leaving, a cushion slipped out from under her clothes. "The other ladies sent up a howl," wrote Mrs. Terasaki, "and the poor woman broke into tears, explaining that besides seven small children to take care of she had her mother-in-law, who was 90, on her hands. We all had a good laugh, but in the future, pregnant women were expertly scrutinized."

Rations also were claimed for a "ghost population" of deceased uncles and aunts, servants who had long since departed and student boarders who had not been seen recently—if ever. Indeed the number of rations issued for nonexistent citizens grew to an estimated one million despite repeated threats by the police and the Ministry of Justice to jail any neighborhood captain who tolerated abuses.

Inevitably, the shortages also led to a lively black market in practically everything—particularly perishable foods, which often were unavailable through official channels. The black marketeers included not only professional criminals, but others who had never before defied the law; unabashedly, they bought up scarce commodities and resold them at astronomical prices. In 1943, half of the 2,000 households in one survey were buying some food on the black market. A year later, Tokyo residents had come to rely on the underground market for one tenth of their rice, one third of their fish and two thirds of their fresh vegetables.

Black-market patrons paid dearly for every morsel. By March 1944, most black-market prices were 10 times higher than the official ceiling, and rice was selling for 14 times the government price; by November of the same year, rice was selling at 44 times the official price—and still rising. A bar of toilet soap, officially priced at one tenth of a yen (2.3 cents), fetched a black-market price of 20 yen ($4.60). An eight-pound bag of sugar sold for 3.75 yen (86 cents) through official channels, but as the Allied naval blockade interrupted sugar imports from Taiwan, the price skyrocketed to 1,000 yen ($230) on the black market.

Patrons of the black market ran a number of risks. They had no guarantee of getting what they had paid for, and they could not complain, since dealing on the black market was a crime for the buyer as well as the seller. With each purchase, the buyer had to be wary of a special police unit—the Keizai Keisatsu, or Economic Police—created to confiscate illegal goods and prosecute offenders.

Gwen Terasaki was one black-market patron who did not get what she bought. A fly-by-night operator came to her home selling rentan—small sawdust, coal and charcoal briquettes, which the Japanese burned in portable braziers to heat their homes. The dealer said that as his briquettes had just been made and were still heavy with moisture, he would give her a sizable reduction in the inflated black-market price. Mrs. Terasaki, not one to pass up a bargain, bought his whole wagonload of rentan and carefully laid out each briquette in her garden to dry. Instead of hardening into precious fuel as they dried, however, the briquettes crumbled into the fine black mud from which they had been shaped. By then, of course, the dealer was long gone.

Japan's elite, of course, did not have to deal with black-market operators or stand in ration lines. Members of the privileged class—senior military officers, high-ranking bureaucrats and industrialists—used their influence to keep their houses stocked with food, wine and other scarce goods. They dined in restaurants closed to the general public and continued to patronize the big cities' geisha houses, bars and brothels. As late as 1944, upper-class households still employed 600,000 maids and other servants.

As ration lines lengthened, the less-fortunate civilians grew increasingly resentful of the wealthy and powerful. By 1943, a complaint was making the rounds: "Everything goes to the military, the black market and the big shots. Only the fools queue up." The arrogant, high-living officer corps bore the brunt of the criticism, particularly after news of military defeats at last began filtering back to the home islands. "People said that they would not begrudge special privileges to a victorious Army and Navy," reported journalist Masuo Kato, "but losers should not expect preferential treatment."

Those who could not afford black-market prices had to get what they needed by improvising. Housewives used flints to light their kitchen fires after their daily ration of four matches had been used up; they began cooking their meals

over a fire of glowing, oil-rich pine cones. Smokers supplemented their daily ration of six cigarettes by smoking dried and shredded eggplant or persimmon leaves rolled in pages torn from pocket-sized books. Connoisseurs of sake, the fermented rice wine, struggled to accustom their palates to a vulgar substitute made from more plentiful sweet potatoes. The potato liquor was so potent that a shot of it earned the nickname *bakudan,* or bombshell.

Housewives who could not afford black-market laundry soap washed their clothes with a mixture made of lye and the pods of the honey-locust tree. Bleach had all but disappeared from the market shelves, and at least one innovative woman added nightingale droppings—a natural whitener—to her hot laundry water. A substitute for toilet soap was a small bran-filled muslin sack.

Some Japanese managed to find humor in the shortages. A bemused citizen pronounced soaplessness a blessing in a satirical article entitled "Vitamin D Is Lost through Baths." For the government, however, the problem of keeping its citizens clean was no laughing matter. When the shortage of fuel threatened to close down many of Tokyo's public bathhouses in early 1944, the city assembly met in emergency session to discuss the problem.

The city fathers decided that bathing was so important to public health and psychological well-being that bathhouses must remain open at any cost. Members of the neighborhood associations were sent out on special hunts for bathhouse firewood, and patrons of each local bathhouse were urged to donate their old clogs to fuel its fires. The bathhouse proprietor was held responsible for keeping his customers satisfied. If he failed, the police were empowered to replace him with someone who could keep the water hot.

Although Japan was poor in most natural resources, especially oil, iron ore and rubber, the nation entered the War with an abundant pool of first-class labor. Japanese workers were diligent and deeply committed to the success of their companies, putting in regular 10-hour shifts without stoppages or strikes. Japanese industry had adopted a paternalistic attitude toward its labor force; companies looked after the health, education and recreation of workers and their families. As a result, unions had not been an important factor in prewar Japan, and by 1942, government edicts had eliminated all national organizations representing the interests of workers in the factories or on the farms.

But for all its efficiency and loyalty, Japanese labor failed to meet the nation's wartime needs. This failure was largely the fault of the government, which never managed to centralize economic planning and production. The result was a hodgepodge of conflicting policies and orders that stifled initiative, undercut production and reduced large segments of the labor force almost to the status of slaves.

At the root of the problem lay a lack of cooperation among the government agencies responsible for war production and military manpower. The military authorities, steeped in the ancient samurai belief that every man was first a warrior, indiscriminately drafted the critical workers who kept Japan's industry functioning: engineers, electronics technicians, foremen, machinists and skilled carpenters.

By September 1943, three million factory workers had been drafted into the armed forces, and the loss had cut severely into the output of aircraft plants, shipyards and munitions factories. "Our technicians were spread too thin to be effective in maintaining standards," said an executive of the big Hitachi electrical company. "We lost 1,000 skilled workers and it took 4,000 unskilled workers to replace them." Managers encountered similar problems when they attempted to expand traditional 10-hour, one-shift factory operations to round-the-clock production. The second shift had to be abandoned in at least one vital electronics plant because the unskilled night workers spoiled more items than they produced.

Production problems were exacerbated by the fact that many of the larger assembly plants depended on a steady supply of small parts from hundreds of tiny firms, many of them employing only two or three technicians. When a single key worker was drafted from one of these supplier firms, its entire production might come to a halt.

Every bit as harmful to war production was the meddling of the military. Both the Army and Navy assigned junior officers, most of them with no experience in business or industry, to supervise factories producing such crucial items as airplane parts, marine engines and gun sights. "These junior officers," Masuo Kato later wrote, "developed into so many little Tojos in their own spheres, making unreasonable and coercive demands."

"Make your life frugal," urges the message emblazoned on this home-front poster, and "waste not even one nail." The latter injunction was hardly necessary: Nails were in such short supply that often the only way to obtain them was to pull them out of existing structures.

Goaded by these unwanted overseers, factory managers struggled to meet increasing quotas of ships, planes and guns. Inevitably, quality suffered. At the Mitsubishi aircraft plant near Nagoya, hastily built airplanes came out of the factory on carts drawn by oxen. Conditions were almost as primitive at a Nakajima plant that was ordered to double its production of airplane engines between September 1943 and March 1944. "To achieve that goal," said the company president, Chikuhei Nakajima, "we mobilized all our material and resources. But after March, parts and material were exhausted and machines worn out. Skilled mechanics were drafted and replaced by school children."

The results were predictable. By the end of 1944, about two thirds of Japan's new fighter planes were breaking down before they reached a combat zone. The Ki 84, a type of Army fighter built by Nakajima, proved to be so flawed that it earned the grim sobriquet "Pilot Killer."

The government scrambled desperately to replace workers conscripted into the services. To make workers available, plants and shops producing nonessential goods were shut down. The labor policy that eventually emerged was a curious mix of incentive and coercion. On the one hand, men were encouraged to volunteer for such difficult and critical work as coal mining and stevedoring by the promise of extra rations, additional pay and three liters of sake per month. On the other hand, a labor draft was instituted primarily to intimidate people into volunteering.

All men between the ages of 16 and 40 were required to register with the government for conscription into war industry. Early in 1944, the registration requirement was ex-

panded to include all males aged 12 through 59. Actually, only 1.5 million men received the labor service's dreaded white conscription notice, and many of them avoided a possible assignment to a war plant far from home by quickly taking a job in a local factory.

Among the emergency workers in war industry were hundreds of thousands of women. Housewives and schoolgirls alike volunteered to help the war effort. Some women figuratively stepped into their husbands' shoes: When Ayame Shimoda's husband was drafted, she took up his miner's pick and reported to his coal mine, ready for work.

Although women were never conscripted, they came under relentless pressure to volunteer. For some of them, work in the war plants was simply too hard—and conditions grew steadily worse. Days off dwindled to three a month; the work day was lengthened to 12 hours, then to 13 hours, and finally was left to the employer's discretion, which meant that work went on until production quotas were met. To save the time spent commuting, many workers took to living in the factories, spreading their sleeping mats on the floor a few feet away from the assembly lines.

The toil, the tedium and the regimentation were almost too much for Hiroko Nakamoto, a schoolgirl who worked in an aircraft-parts plant in Hiroshima. "On the night shift," she recalled, "after standing up for hours, we were marched into a dining hall where we had our supper. Supper was a bowl of weak, hot broth, usually with one string of noodle in it and a few soybeans at the bottom. We would gulp it down, then go back to the factory."

With winter coming on, Hiroko and her shift worked in the cold—there was no fuel available for heat. "Finally a few empty oil cans were brought in, and small pieces of charcoal were burned in them. Seeing the glow of the little pieces of charcoal, smelling the smoke, we felt warmer.

"At 11 o'clock, we went to the dormitory. We were supposed to go quietly to bed. But suddenly our long hours of discipline and self-control were ended. We could not be quiet. We stamped our feet and yelled and jumped up and down. We played our harmonicas and sang at the top of our voices. The manager of the factory would come in and roar: 'Quiet! Stop that noise!' We would then sing even louder. I think we were a little crazy."

The workers were poorly paid and they lost ground stead-

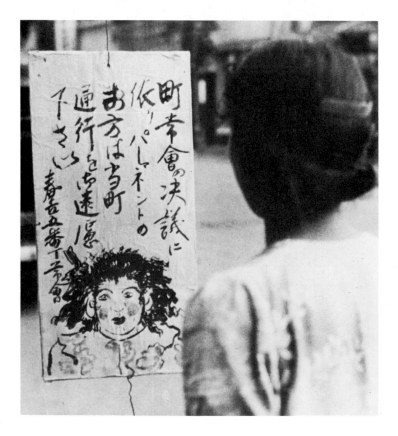

"Women with permanent waves will please refrain from passing through here," cautions this placard put up by a zealous neighborhood association. To eliminate extravagant Western-style hairdos, the Japanese government limited hairdressers to three curls per customer.

Two workmen watch giant automated rollers—imported from the United States—turn out sheet steel in a plant near Tokyo. Although the Japanese boasted of their self-sufficient industries, more than 90 per cent of their machine tools actually had been imported before the War.

ily to inflation. The government had frozen wages and prices at 1939 levels, but the shortages and the increasing flow of essential goods to the black market soon made the price freeze meaningless. Slowly, wages were allowed to rise, but the cost of living for Japanese families increased by at least 20 per cent each year of the War.

Despite rising prices, more and more money was siphoned out of the workers' pockets to finance the War. Income taxes, withheld from a worker's pay by his employer, increased from 10 per cent in 1942 to 15 per cent in 1944. Anyone who earned more than 3,000 yen per year—approximately $690—was subject to a special surtax ranging up to 50 per cent. The biggest bite of all was taken by the government's national savings and bond-purchase plans, to which the average worker was expected to divert 20 per cent of his or her salary. The investments were solicited by the neighborhood associations, whose captains made repeated appeals and sometimes thinly veiled threats in order to meet their government-assigned quotas.

Money deposited in the savings program could be withdrawn only with the permission of the neighborhood association, and then only for emergencies. The government

bonds were supposed to be negotiable, but many could not be redeemed because the certificates themselves had never been issued. The official explanation was that an acute shortage of paper prevented the government from printing the bonds. Quite possibly the buyers' funds were being deliberately frozen out of their reach.

Many Japanese quietly rebelled against these conditions by staying away from their jobs as often as they could. In some factories, the absentee rate rose to 25 per cent of the work force. Many workers took unofficial leaves in the spring and in the fall so that they could return to the farm to help with the planting and harvesting. Some workers took time off to handle family affairs and household chores, while others stayed home when breakdowns in the public transportation system forced them to walk or bicycle long distances to their jobs.

For some workers, protest was impossible. These unfortunates were the 667,000 Koreans and 38,000 Chinese who had come to Japan on two-year labor contracts and had ended up as slave laborers. During the day, they worked under armed guard at the hardest and most dangerous jobs: stevedoring, heavy construction, steel manufac-

turing and coal mining. Then at night, they were locked in isolated compounds, some of which were surrounded by electrified barbed-wire fences. When their contracts expired, the foreign laborers were told that no shipping was available to take them home; they were trapped in Japan for the duration of the War.

The Koreans were abused by their Japanese guards, but they were saved from worse treatment by the fact that they were legal subjects of the Empire. The worst was reserved for the Chinese. "The kinder the Chinese are treated," Japanese supervisors were told by the police, "the more demanding and impudent they become. Therefore, neither leniency nor generosity is necessary."

Most supervisors took the advice to heart. They beat the Chinese with wooden clubs when they failed to understand orders spoken in Japanese, and battered them into senselessness if they tried to escape the brutal treatment. When a fire in the Miike coal mine trapped several dozen Chinese miners in a shaft, the manager did not bother to attempt their rescue. The shaft entrance was sealed shut, and work resumed elsewhere as if nothing had happened. It turned out that 13 Japanese also perished in the fire.

Besides the grim toll taken by beatings and accidents, many Chinese and Koreans were simply worked to death. More than 60,000 Koreans were estimated to have died in Japanese custody. Among the Chinese workers, the death toll was 7,000—more than 17 per cent of the total.

Among the dead were 418 of the 850 Chinese who worked at the Hanaoka copper mine in northern Honshu. Unable to bear the harsh treatment and inhuman living conditions any longer, these workers rebelled in June of 1945. The police put down the rebellion with all necessary force—and then some. Most of the men who perished were flogged to death.

There were many fatalities among Japanese workers as well; disease and fatigue caused by long hours in unsafe and unhealthy workplaces took a heavy toll. The number of industrial accidents rose steadily. Poor sanitation led to dysentery, typhus and typhoid fever. Malnutrition brought on epidemics of painful and disabling beriberi; the manager of the Mitsubishi glass factory in Tsurumi discovered that 30 per cent of the women and boys in his plant suffered from the disease. The crowded living conditions and dank factories caused an alarming increase in tuberculosis, which killed more than 170,000 Japanese in 1943 alone.

The victims could expect little help: Doctors and hospitals were short on antiseptics, blood plasma, serums, sulfa drugs and vaccines, a result of military appropriations and the Allied blockade of raw materials. In fact, many hospitals became health hazards themselves. Sanitary standards deteriorated dangerously as the number of doctors and nurses decreased; medical techniques became more and more primitive as equipment wore out. Surgical dressings had to be washed and reused repeatedly. The drug shortage became so critical that civilians were urged to grow medicinal herbs to supplement the commercial drug supply.

Fully four fifths of Japan's psychiatric institutions were forced to close down as a result of shortages of trained personnel. But, despite the subsequent lack of psychological counseling and treatment, and despite the terrible stresses and strains of wartime living, Japan's suicide rate declined each year. It seemed that full employment and dedication to the war effort helped people to neutralize their personal fears and anxieties.

An attendant fuels an automobile (right) at one of the charcoal stations that appeared in Japan as gasoline became scarce and cars were converted to burn solids. As wood to make charcoal became scarce in turn, more exotic fuels were concocted. At left, a technician loads a fuel brick into a car before taking it for a successful test drive. The brick was made by blending household garbage with coal dust and heavy oil residue, and then baking the mixture into a solid.

The War brought new hardships to Japan's 14 million farmers and farmworkers, whose social and economic position was fairly well described by a cynical old Japanese saying: "Farmers should neither live nor die." Farm families subsisted on plots that averaged only 2.5 acres, many of which were leased from wealthy landowners at exorbitant rents. "They tell us, 'Deliver! Deliver!' " complained one farmer, "and then they come and take away at a song the rice we sweated so hard to produce."

Farmers had to work harder and longer to keep up their prewar output of grains and vegetables. The backbone of the rural labor force, 2.8 million young men and 650,000 young women, had left the farm for the armed forces or the war plants. The military requisitioned most farm horses early in the War, and there were only 99 tractors left in all of Japan by 1942. Shortages of chemical fertilizers and the effects of two unusually cold winters further reduced the nation's crop yields.

Most of the farm work fell to the farmers' wives, mothers, sisters and grandparents. Children and adolescents helped with the weeding and other farm chores during their summer vacations and school holidays. Of course, some of the youngsters did not take the work seriously. "Farmers are complaining," reported a Yokohama newspaper in June 1942, "that the high-school students who are supposed to help them with the barley harvest often treat the work as play. They do not display much love of farming."

Nevertheless, school children played an increasingly important role in farming as the labor shortage worsened. By October of 1944, many of the two million children who had been mobilized into volunteer units worked on farms. Sometimes entire city schools moved to the countryside, where the hard-pressed teachers attempted to squeeze in classes after long days in the fields.

Beginning in 1943, the government put even more pressure on the farmers by demanding specific quotas of rice, wheat, barley and potatoes. The quotas did not allow for bad harvests due to illness, weather or fertilizer shortages. Farmers with low yields were put in the sorry position of having to turn over their entire crop to the government and then having to apply for rations to feed their families.

In response to this bureaucratic extortion, farmers began holding back increasing quantities of their crops from the rationing authorities. Thus a vicious cycle took hold: The food hoarded by the farmers reduced the amount available through official channels, forcing city residents to buy directly from the farmers. Prices rose, the value of money eroded and the farmers began demanding clothing, kitchen utensils, tobacco and other scarce commodities in exchange for their produce.

On weekends, heavily laden city people jammed the roads and railways, heading for the country to barter their possessions for turnips, cabbages, sweet potatoes and rice. A Tokyo middle-school student watched in dismay as her family traded away its treasured possessions for food. "First we ate my mother's wedding gown," she said. "Then we ate the bicycle. Then the sewing machine. Then we looked around and said: 'What else can we eat?'"

The Economic Police attempted to halt the growing barter economy, since it undercut the official rationing system. Citizens caught dealing on the black market could be charged with any or all of three offenses: paying more than the official price, obtaining more than the official ration, or transporting illegally procured food. The police in the areas to the east of Tokyo were rumored to be strict, so most residents of that city headed for country towns to the north and west. And most of the bartering was done by women, since they seemed to have more luck talking their way out of trouble if the police stopped them on the way home.

The barter system fueled a traditional antagonism between the urban and rural populations, which tended to blame each other for their litany of woe. "City dwellers," wrote journalist Kato, "resented having to go furtively to the countryside with a rucksack to bargain for enough food to stay alive." In turn, some farmers believed that the city people were living high on the hog and could afford to pay. "When we occasionally visited Tokyo," said a farmer in 1943, "people would be gathered in a huge crowd in front of the kabuki theater trying to buy tickets. We could not bear the idea of sweating so hard to produce rice for city people who amused themselves like this."

Few people in Japan were quite so puritanical about commercial amusement, especially traditional kabuki. Entertainment was an essential relief from the pressures of wartime life, and Tokyo residents were not the only ones who flocked to see their favorite actors, dressed in brilliant costumes, moving through exquisitely choreographed steps while speaking lilting poetry. The government, recognizing that kabuki was a tonic for civilian morale, put the show on the road. One troupe, led by the acclaimed performer Kikugoro Onoe, delighted audiences in provincial theaters, factory auditoriums and mining camps.

Because kabuki occupied a hallowed place in Japan's cultural life, the shows continued right up to the end of the War. But almost every other cultural activity was changed, cut back or eliminated. Various art forms were doctored with heavy doses of propaganda intended to steel the people to the hardships ahead. In March 1944, four members of a ballet troupe staged a performance entitled "Decisive Aerial Warfare Ballet." The new work, according to the advertisements, was a contribution to the "national drive to heighten the air consciousness of the people." It was, in fact, a tentative suggestion of the possibility of American air raids—a possibility that became ever more likely as the U.S. island-hopping campaign established air bases closer and closer to Japan.

Japan's heavy-handed censors persisted in war-long efforts to eliminate Western influence from popular culture. Occidental music, which was particularly popular with Japanese youngsters, came under strong attack from the censors. Jazz was banned from the radio and the tenor saxophone was labeled a tool of the enemy. The Japan Victor Recording Company was forced to change its name to Nippon Onkyo (Japan Sound) and remove the English words "His Master's Voice" from the company trademark. The police were enlisted in a campaign to round up all copies of British and American records previously marketed in Japan. Despite fervent appeals to the patriotism of music lovers, however, the police obtained very few records voluntarily from collectors.

Motion pictures remained the most popular form of mass entertainment. Of course, nearly all films made in Allied countries were banned, to the intense disappointment of fans who had been waiting eagerly for the Tokyo opening of the much-publicized American Civil War epic, *Gone with the Wind.* One exception to the ban was the movie *Mr. Smith Goes to Washington,* which starred actor James Stewart as a U.S. senator who filibusters against corrupt power brokers. The Japanese censors passed the film on the ground that it showed the degeneracy of American democracy.

Japanese film makers produced a spate of routine propaganda movies glorifying the military and Japan's great victories early in the War. But by 1944, shortages of technicians and equipment had brought film production to a virtual halt. Fans found it more and more difficult to see even a rerun, for movie theaters were ordered to put on no more than three shows a day to save fuel.

By a stroke of luck, a print of *Gone with the Wind* was seized by Japanese troops during the capture of Singapore in February 1942 and was sent to a propaganda unit in Tokyo. Though the movie was never shown to the wartime public, a young diplomat named Norizane Ikeda saw it at a private screening. "I felt strangely depressed," he said, "when I saw the Yankees attacking the South. I was thinking how terrible it would be if Tokyo burned like Atlanta."

The censors made no attempt to abolish the imported game of baseball but they did naturalize it with some distinctively Japanese touches. In play-by-play broadcasts, sports announcers substituted Japanese-sounding words for the familiar terms derived from English. Radio listeners had trouble following the game until they learned that a *sutoraiku,* or strike, was now a *honkyu;* that a *boru,* or ball, had become a *gaikyu;* and that *hitto endo ran*—hit and run—had lost out to *kyosoda.*

Like everything else, the quality of professional baseball declined as the better athletes were drafted into the Army and Navy. By 1944, so few players were left that the league suspended play in midseason and the Osaka Tigers were declared the champions. The oldest baseball field in Japan was plowed and planted with vegetables to feed Yokohama's hungry population.

The sport least affected by the War was sumo, the ancient Japanese form of wrestling. The beefy performers, who weighed from 250 to 300 pounds, occasionally donned uniforms and went on recruitment drives. But the master wrestlers were excused from the draft and continued to clash in tests of brute strength at Tokyo's outdoor Korakuen Stadium.

Fans of sumo, including Prime Minister Tojo, flocked to see Futabayama, who was the reigning champion when Japan entered the War. By 1943, however, the great Futabayama had begun to lose some bouts. Some of his fans saw this as an omen of impending defeat for the nation.

One by one, the War did away with the simple pleasures of life. Tokyo's famous Hibiya Park was closed to strollers, although no one could offer a reason for this restriction. People who liked to go fishing on a day off could no longer make a meal of their day's catch; they were required to turn in whatever fish they caught to Army or Navy food centers. New reading material became increasingly hard to find as printers were drafted, paper and printer's ink were rationed, and independent-minded writers were hounded into inactivity by the censors. The number of new book titles published plummeted from 28,138 in 1941 to about 5,300 in 1942. The number of magazines published dropped from 1,970 in 1940 to fewer than 1,000 in 1944, and the press-run of each issue was drastically reduced.

And so, in ways subtle and profound, life had become sad even when there were no casualty lists to make it tragic. A father, anguished to watch his child suffer through the winter without enough clothes to keep warm, wrote a brief poem: "Putting my child's frostbitten hand in my own, I almost dropped tears on it." Another father wrote about his nightly vigil: "There was the quiet sound of an iron kettle boiling water late at night, as I waited for my child working in a factory." The special Japanese sensitivity to beauty survived, but it too was tinctured with sadness. A sick girl who received a lovely red apple as a gift said, "I just put it at my bedside for three days."

Except for grief and hope, emotions were blunted in the constant struggle to work and survive. "Love-making was impossible," recalled a young Osaka woman who toiled in a war plant. Dissenters who deplored the War—and especially the Tojo government's conduct of the War—seldom risked speaking up, and in time their anger subsided to bleak despair. People felt awash in the cold gloom that a newly drafted college student described in a letter to a friend: "If I survive"—and he would not—"there will be a time when I can talk to you about this long, long night, this unending, starless black void."

TOO LITTLE OF EVERYTHING

A donkey-drawn delivery cart, pressed into service when fuel began to run short, captures the attention of passersby in Tokyo's fashionable Ginza district.

"SUDDENLY THE STORES ALL BECAME EMPTY"

Civilians eat zosui—a weak vegetable stew—at a government-run dining hall, one of hundreds that opened as rationing forced restaurants to close.

When Kenzo Nakajima, a well-known writer serving with the Japanese Army, came home on leave from Malaya in 1943, he was shocked to discover that conditions in Japan were worse than those he had left behind. "Prices were higher," he wrote, "and the black market had become outrageous." Cities that Kenzo remembered as having been bright and bustling now looked drab and down at the heels. People who once had been healthy and happy were now grim and gaunt; they were enduring privation and disease to keep the servicemen clothed and fed. "Every Japanese," observed a foreign diplomat, "acts as though he carries the whole responsibility for victory on his own shoulders."

The effects of shortages were visible everywhere. Automobile and truck engines stalled when drivers tried to use soybean oil as a substitute for scarce petroleum lubricants. Elevators powered by electricity stopped running. New buildings collapsed because too much sand had been used to stretch the supply of cement. Housewives spent entire days searching for such common items as buttons, socks, matches and toilet paper. In 1943 some 11,000 Tokyo shops had to shut their doors for lack of merchandise or help. "The invisible hand of a magician seemed to move," said a Yokohama schoolteacher, "and suddenly the stores all became empty."

Hunger was everywhere—constant, gnawing hunger that sapped the people's strength and ruined their health. Government rations provided only half the food value of the standard prewar diet. Often, the makeshift official ration of unhusked rice and other coarse grains caused entire families to fall sick because their digestive systems were unable to tolerate the excessive roughage.

The civilians endured. They ate thistle, mugwort and chickweed—anything that grew. They gathered acorns and ground them into flour. They captured stray cats and dogs and slaughtered them for table meat. "Only when you were very hungry," said a Tokyo high-school girl, "did you think back on all the food you used to have and wonder silently when will we get that again?"

Young volunteers plant rice seedlings in Tokyo's Ueno Park. By February of 1945, three million school-aged youngsters had joined the national labor force.

In the rugged, mist-shrouded hills to the north of Tokyo, priests of the local Sanpo Shrine break new ground to wrest a garden plot from land previously considered unarable.

A mother and her sons feed their hens dried grasshoppers.

VICTORY GARDENS, JAPANESE-STYLE

To stave off the growing threat of famine, the Japanese used every inch of arable land. They plowed up baseball fields and schoolyards and planted grain and vegetables. They dug garden plots on golf courses, and golfers had to do a little cultivating before teeing off. Citizens of Yokohama planted pumpkins along the main boulevards, and Tokyo residents grew turnips in the boxes of earth they kept at the ready to snuff out incendiary bombs.

To make new farmland, schoolteacher Masako Ando led 600 pupils from Nagoya into the mountains, where they spent 13 days pulling out rocks and tree stumps. "I was so tired that my hoe dropped," she said later. "I forget whether all of this had any effect on the War."

Transforming the steep hillsides into productive land, a farm family plants rice seedlings in tiny paddies on terraces that are accessible only by ladders.

Buddhist monks donate the temple's metal gongs, urns, vases and candlesticks to the scrap drive.

Tokyo youngsters pile a handcart with salvaged meta

Volunteers redeem aluminum coins for use in aircraft.

Members of a neighborhood association cull tiny pieces of iron from a factory's metal waste

POTS AND PANS FOR WAGING WAR

Salvaging quantities of precious metal, schoolgirls pull silver and gold threads from kimonos.

Children turn in plastic and metal toys to be recycled.

Tokyo merchants donate old bicycles and spare parts.

Families in Hiroshima contribute household utensils and knickknacks to the nationwide drive.

To relieve critical shortages of the metals and alloys needed for military production, the Japanese government launched an unrelenting nationwide scrap drive. Big cities offered the best pickings. Tokyo was stripped of ornamental iron street lamps, railings, brass traffic-lane markers, building plaques and the decorative metal on its bridges. Iron benches were ripped out of city parks and rail stations. Even the bronze gates to Tokyo's Yasukuni Shrine for the war dead were dismantled and shipped to a munitions factory.

Shinto shrines donated their brass lanterns, Buddhist temples their great gongs. A Yokohama museum that had been established to commemorate the disastrous 1923 earthquake donated 10 tons of exhibits, including twisted streetcar rails and broken metal water pipes.

Housewives turned in utensils by the thousands and everyone traded his aluminum yen for newly minted tin coins. When heating fuel ran out, office managers tore out their buildings' radiators.

By 1944, the aluminum shortage had become so serious that units of military police were mobilized for the scrap drive, and each family was allowed only one pot for cooking and one pail for hauling water.

Beating the transportation shortage, officials distribute fresh radishes from a requisitioned streetcar.

MAKING THE BEST OF
THE TRANSPORT CRISIS

For many Japanese, the task of getting to work and home again became a daily battle. As taxis, cars and buses were immobilized by the lack of fuel and spare parts, commuters crowded into trains and streetcars. But public transportation was itself drastically reduced, ticket prices went up, waiting lines grew longer and longer. In many cities, trains and trolleys were being commandeered to transport military personnel and essential goods.

Left to their own devices, commuters rode bicycles—until the tires wore out and no replacements could be found. Finally, there was nothing left but to walk—to struggle along exhaustingly in the clumsy wooden clogs that had replaced shoes.

Broken-down buses, neatly aligned in a makeshift encampment, are put to use as shelters for city families whose homes have been destroyed by bombs.

WOMEN'S WORK

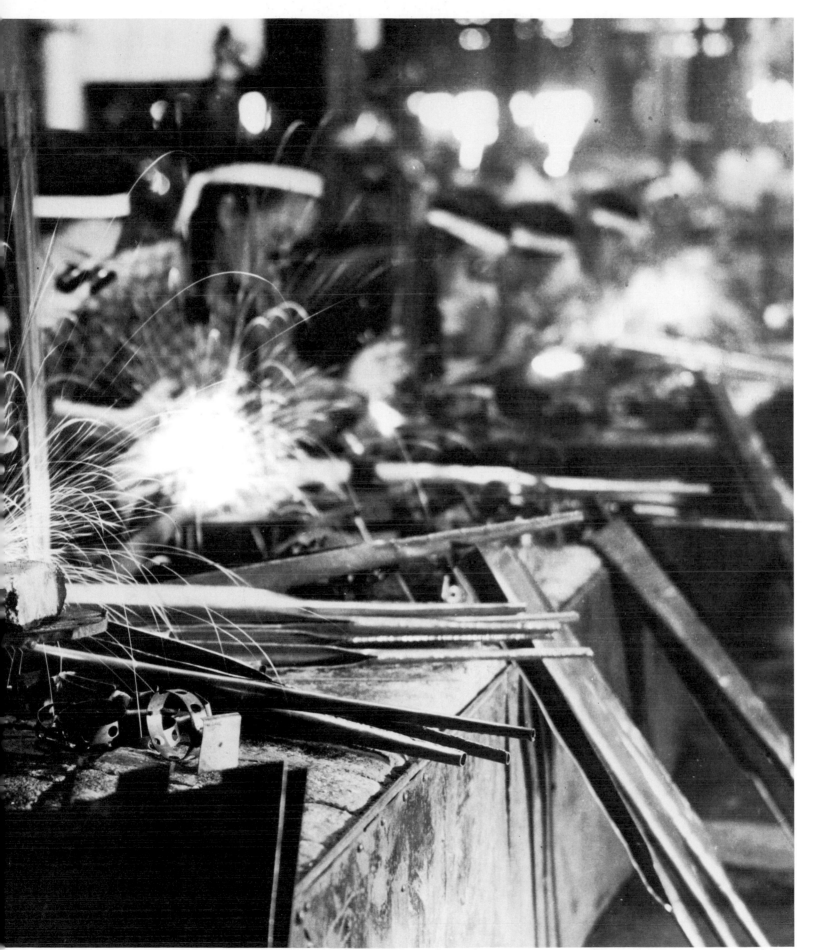

Women welders—among the four million of their sex working in Japanese war industries by 1944—operate acetylene torches on an aircraft assembly line.

VITAL REPLACEMENTS FOR LOST MANPOWER

"The enemy is drafting women," Welfare Minister Chika-hiko Koizumi proclaimed erroneously in 1942. "But in Japan, out of consideration for the family system, we will not draft them." Prime Minister Tojo went even further: "We are able to do our duties only because we have wives and mothers at home."

Such was the traditional view of the woman's place in Japanese society. It was acceptable for unmarried young women to work in textiles, to teach and to serve as nurses. But once a marriage was arranged, they were expected to quit work and concentrate on raising a family.

By the summer of 1943, however, tradition had fallen victim to increasing military needs. The government policy became "men to the front, women to the workplace." All over Japan, women took a variety of jobs formerly done by men: bus driver, clerk, ticket taker, barber, cook and salesperson.

A few months later, the government announced that unmarried females between the ages of 12 and 39 must register for a possible labor draft and that a new organization, the Women's Volunteer Labor Corps, would help staff the war plants. Women were not required to join the corps, which entailed a year's duty in a factory. But the neighborhood associations heckled shirkers as "unpatriotic" and "women of leisure," and they kept the plants filled with volunteers—among them, one of Tojo's daughters.

Once the traditional barriers had fallen, Japanese women and schoolgirls performed hard and sometimes dangerous physical labor in coal mines and steel mills. By 1944, more than 14 million women had become wage earners. They worked alongside the few undrafted male technicians and shared their hardships: 12- to 16-hour shifts in unheated factories. "When we worked nights," one girl recalled, "we had to sleep in the factory. We could go home the next morning, just so we were back in the factory by 3 o'clock."

Despite the hardships, many of the women were delighted with their new status. Said a popular women's magazine with pride and perhaps a trace of surprise: "Japanese women should no longer be thought of as playthings."

Working at a textile plant, women pack and mark bales of raw silk—one of the few jobs deemed appropriate for women before the War.

A group of women and schoolgirls—glorified with the title of "production-increase troops"—turns out simple aircraft parts in a small Tokyo factory.

ON-THE-JOB TRAINING FOR SCHOOLGIRLS

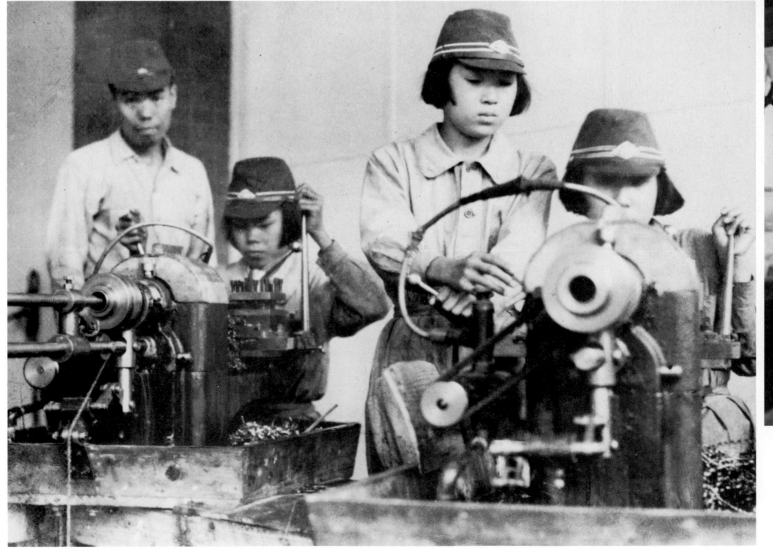

Girls in a Tokyo high-school class watch a teacher show how to fashion hospital robes for convalescent soldiers. The students, wearing masks to avoid contaminating the robes, spent class time each day sewing the garments. In some schools, light machinery or simple assembly lines were set up—and study time was reduced to only two hours per day.

Three girl students, attended by their instructor, practice the technique of operating a lathe. The inexperienced new workers could not match the output of the men they replaced; a manufacturer complained that "three workers were doing the same work that one had done in 1940."

MONOTONOUS HOURS OF MENIAL LABOR

MONOTONOUS HOURS OF MENIAL LABOR

Women paste together cement sacks in a dimly lit factory north of Tokyo. There was little relief from such drab tasks: Factory workers usually toiled at least 12 hours daily and were accorded only two days off per month. In time even the two rest days were eliminated.

Women volunteers shoulder crates at a port on Karafuto (Sakhalin Island), at that time one of Japan's northernmost territories. As the demand for laborers increased, the laws protecting women from long hours or strenuous labor were relaxed or suspended.

PRISONERS OF THE PRODUCTION LINE

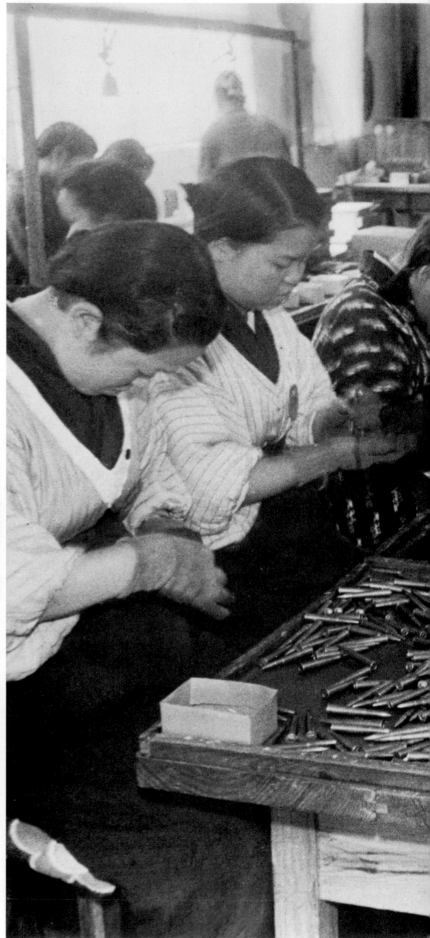

Huddled beneath quilts, men and women workers sleep while in the background another shift toils on the noisy assembly line of an aircraft-production plant on Kyushu. Laborers who became ill on the job were, as a rule, instructed to "carry on for the sake of the country."

Women inspect machine-gun cartridges in a Tokyo armaments factory. In spite of the hazards of working with munitions, women seldom were paid more than half the wage earned by the men they had replaced.

4

On the afternoon of May 21, 1943, Tokyo radio made a somber announcement: "Admiral Yamamoto, while directing general strategy in the front line in April of this year, engaged in combat with the enemy and met gallant death in a warplane." Then the announcer broke down and wept.

Much of Japan wept with him. Isoroku Yamamoto had been his nation's greatest warrior: planner and executor of the daring attack on Pearl Harbor, father of Japan's naval air arm, which was responsible for sinking the British battleships *Prince of Wales* and *Repulse*. Now, by virtue of his heroic death, Yamamoto had become a *kami*—a god.

The day after his death was made public, the Cabinet Information Bureau announced that Yamamoto had been promoted to fleet admiral and had been awarded the Collar of the Supreme Order of the Chrysanthemum—Japan's highest decoration. And he was to be honored with a state funeral—only the 12th such ceremony in the nation's history.

On June 5, hundreds of thousands of citizens lined the streets of Tokyo to pay homage to Yamamoto. One thousand five hundred official mourners gathered at the Navy Club, where the admiral's ashes had lain in state for two weeks. At 8:50 that morning, crewmen from Yamamoto's flagship, the *Musashi,* carried his ashes to a black gun carriage outside the club. Then, to the strains of Chopin's "Funeral March," the mourners marched slowly to Hibiya Park in the center of Tokyo.

Three pavilions had been constructed at the park to serve as a Shinto shrine. Inside the center pavilion an altar of unvarnished wood, with black-and-white curtains, had been erected. A vase of red roses, sent by Italian dictator Benito Mussolini, gave the scene its only touch of color.

Representatives of the Imperial Family paid their respects before the altar; the Emperor himself did not attend, for custom dictated that he must remain remote and sequestered. The chief officiant, Admiral Koichi Shiozawa, a lifelong friend of the hero, commended Yamamoto's spirit to the Yasukuni Shrine, where the souls of Japan's war dead were believed to reside. As Yamamoto's eldest son, 22-year-old Yoshimasa, stepped forward to offer a sprig from Shinto's sacred evergreen, the *sakaki,* a Navy band played the ceremonial march "Casting My Life Aside."

That afternoon, Tokyo's citizens passed by the altar in final tribute. In the evening, half of Yamamoto's ashes were

THE MILITARY LIFE

placed in a white box six inches square and interred at the Tama Cemetery just outside Tokyo. The rest of the ashes were taken to Yamamoto's home in Nagaoka, 140 miles from Tokyo, and buried near the grave of his father on the grounds of a Zen temple. His gravestone was a plain marker that cost less than 70 yen—$16. The epitaph on it read simply, "Killed in action in the South Pacific, 1943."

Yamamoto had died a hero's death in the best tradition of the nation's samurai past. To be prepared for such a death was the object of every Japanese boy's training.

In primary schools throughout the nation, six-year-old children learned about the importance of the soldier before they learned much else. Wearing their blue school uniforms, they sang a song of thanksgiving that said: "Shoulder to shoulder with my elder brother, / I can go to school today, / Thanks to the soldiers, thanks to the soldiers / Who fought for our country, for our country." One of the first lessons in the "Japanese Reader" began with a picture of three toy soldiers and the caption "Advance, Advance, / Soldiers move forward. / The sun is red, / The rising sun is red. / The flag of the sun! / Banzai! (Long life!)"

Reinforcing such lessons were ceremonies that fostered the patriotic spirit. Portraits of the Emperor and the Empress, kept in a special room in the school in a shrinelike wooden box covered with purple curtains, were taken to the school auditorium on national holidays. There, after the national anthem was sung, the Imperial Rescript on Education was read and the purple curtain was lifted so that students and teachers could bow before the portraits. School children also were taken frequently to Shinto shrines to pay homage to the Emperor.

The children visited nearby Army and Navy bases, and they listened in awe to the soldiers and sailors who came to their schools to give pep talks. When one soldier, Naoki Sakuhara, asked who was willing to give his life for Japan, the entire class stood up even before he had finished asking the question. Journalist Masuo Kato, a worldly man who had lived in Washington, D.C. before the War and took much of the militaristic propaganda with a grain of salt, was shocked when his own son—who was only in elementary school at the time—remarked casually one day: "Daddy, I will die for our country."

Playtime was devoted to martial activities: judo, close-order drill and kendo, a rough form of fencing using bamboo sticks. To toughen the youngsters, instructors ordered them to strip to the waist and then put them through outdoor exercises even in the dead of winter. Anyone who dared to wear a pair of gloves or mittens was called a yowamushi—a weak worm.

Softness and sensitivity were ridiculed or censured. A young boy at a school in the Yamagata district of northern Honshu was severely chastised for crying when told to dissect a frog. The teacher gave him a sharp blow on the head and said: "Why are you crying about one miserable frog? When you grow up, you will have to kill a hundred, two hundred Chinese."

When boys reached middle school at the age of 12 or 13, deeds were joined to words: They were given uniforms and light rifles and hours of military instruction each week. Hillis Lory, an American who taught in Japan before the War, was startled by the intensity and youthfulness of the mock warriors and the verisimilitude of their training exercises. As many as 10,000 students would take part in war games, which lasted two to three days every autumn and covered wide areas of countryside. Said Lory: "The cracking of rifles, the roar of planes overhead, the rumble of the armored cars presented in these battles all the aspects of war."

The curriculum followed a War Ministry directive that "education of a very intellectual type must be abandoned." Literature, history and the arts were de-emphasized, and students were given more scientific and technical courses that would be of practical value to the armed forces or to the war industry. Years later, a wartime student summed up the results: "The teachers were excellent instructors, but they never made us think about anything. We just earnestly memorized everything."

Young men who did not go on to middle school nevertheless got the benefit of a military education while they learned a trade. They enrolled in youth training schools, where the five-year course consisted mostly of military drill and indoctrination.

All students—indeed the entire civilian populace—were fed a steady diet of stories that nourished their martial spirit. Once war began, propagandists published documented accounts of heroism in battle—and occasional stories that defied rational explanation. One such tale described a heroic pilot who temporarily conquered death in order to lead his squadron back to its base. "After the last plane returned," the story went, "he made out a report and proceeded to headquarters. As soon as he had finished his report, he suddenly dropped to the ground.

"The officers on the spot rushed to give assistance but, alas, he was dead. On examining his body they found that it was already cold; he had a bullet wound in his chest that had proved fatal. It is impossible for the body of a newly dead person to be cold. Nevertheless the body of the captain was as cold as ice. He must have died long before, and it was his spirit that made the report. Such a miracle must have been achieved by the strict sense of responsibility that the dead captain possessed."

Nearly all teen-age boys looked forward to their military service, and most got their chance sooner rather than later. In 1941 all men except college students were conscripted at the age of 20. Boys were permitted to volunteer at the age of 17, and later, at 15. On October 2, 1943, after the Allied invasion of New Guinea, the War Ministry decided to draft college students too, exempting only those men studying science or medicine. It was a drastic move in a society that had a high regard for education—but not drastic enough to meet the increased manpower needs of the Army. Less than three months later, the draft age for everyone was lowered to 19, and within six months to 18.

A red postcard notified a Japanese man that he had "the honor to be conscripted into the Army to serve His Majesty, the Emperor." More than 130,000 college students aged 20 or older received such a notice in October 1943. By the end of that year, their induction had helped to increase the size of the armed forces to 3.8 million men—one million more than at the end of 1942.

The draftees were given one month to report for physical examinations. The physicals were usually held in their hometowns so that the young men could conveniently visit the graves of their ancestors. This served as an emotional reminder that once a recruit reported for training, he might never see home again.

Before a man left home for a training camp, his family and friends gathered for a round of sokokai—vigorous marching parties—to say good-by and to urge him on to great feats of patriotism. "No one was allowed to say a word of sorrow or pity," recalled Takaaki Aikawa, a schoolteacher who saw many students off to war. " 'Congratulations!' This was the word we said." The recruit would be feted with a cup of hard-to-get sake and a piece of special fish—or any delicacy that was available.

Aikawa, recalling a party for one of his favorite students, wrote regretfully, "We had nothing except a pouch of dried beans—the ration for that day for my whole family, including three hungry children. When the student heard the clock strike five he rose, and, with a faint smile on his face, said to me in a kind of whisper: 'Well, I must go. Thank you very much for teaching me these past few years. Now I am prepared for my death.' "

After a draftee left for the camp, his family might set a place for him at every meal. The practice was intended to show that the absent serviceman was still a member of the family, and it also served as a prayer for his safe return.

On October 21, 1943, thousands of drafted students from Honshu's colleges and universities gathered in the Outer Gardens of the Meiji Shrine in Tokyo for the biggest send-off of the War. In a cold rain, 35,000 young men, rifles on their shoulders, stood facing a stand filled with 65,000 people—middle-school boys and girls, women's-college students, families and friends.

While standing at attention for three hours, the recruits were bombarded with patriotic rhetoric—all of it broadcast to the nation. Shinshiro Ebashi, who until his induction had been a student at Tokyo Imperial University, set the tone with his speech: "We, of course, do not expect to come back alive as we take up guns and bayonets to embark on our glorious mission of crushing the stubborn enemy. Those of you students whom we are leaving behind will, I am sure, follow in our footsteps in the not-too-distant future and march over our dead bodies to win victory in the Greater East Asia War."

A similar exhortation came from Prime Minister Tojo. "The decisive moment has come," he said, "when one hundred million of us take up battle positions and overcome the hardships confronting our fatherland." Tojo reminded the recruits that the United States and Great Britain were also sending their students to war. "But I do not have a shred of doubt that you will overwhelm them in spirit and in combat capability."

After the rally, the recruits marched through the streets of Tokyo to the plaza facing the Imperial Palace, there to shout "Banzai!" for the Emperor.

One last ceremony awaited the conscripts. After they arrived at their training camps, they listened to officers tell them again of the great honor they had been given in being drafted for the Army or Navy. They were sworn in by their unit commanders and were read the Emperor Meiji's Imperial Rescript to Soldiers and Sailors, which summed up the lessons of duty and patriotism that had been drummed into them from the cradle.

The last point of the rescript contained a warning: "If you do not make simplicity your aim, you will become effeminate and frivolous and acquire fondness for luxurious and extravagant ways. If such an evil once makes its appearance among soldiers and sailors, it will certainly spread like an epidemic, and martial spirit and morale will constantly decline."

In fact, dissipation of any sort was well-nigh impossible for the recruits. For 12 weeks they endured brutal living conditions and training methods designed to make them tough fighting men. Said a Navy recruit: "Seamen weren't even treated like human beings." Another rookie sailor agreed: "The training made human cattle of every one of us—automatons who obeyed without thinking." Recruits in every service were considered expendable, and they were

Escorted by a Naval honor guard, the ashes of Admiral Isoroku Yamamoto, Japan's greatest wartime hero, are carried on a gun carriage toward the pavilions erected for his state funeral in 1943 in Tokyo's Hibiya Park.

125

constantly reminded of the fact by men who had completed their training. Full-fledged soldiers sarcastically called the Army recruits *issen gorin*—one sen, five ren, or less than a penny—which was the cost of their draft card.

The trainees' new home was a two-story creosoted wooden barracks with whitewashed walls adorned with framed maxims exhorting them to fight to the death for the Emperor. They slept on iron cots equipped with straw mattresses, thin blankets and tubular pillows filled with sawdust. A small wooden locker held each man's few personal possessions, usually limited to family pictures and mementoes. Snapshots of all women except relatives were banned, and before magazines were admitted to the camp, pictures of gei-

sha and female movie stars were cut out on the grounds that they might arouse immoral ideas and distract the recruit from learning the business of war.

All recruits were issued the same uniform: a drab, rough-spun, baggy khaki outfit. Many men from the country found even these loose-fitting uniforms uncomfortable—or difficult to figure out. "I noticed a country boy in the corner of the barracks struggling with his newly issued uniform," noted one officer. "Until that moment he had never worn anything but a loose kimono. When I came up to him, he had his trousers on backward. He was in tears because he could not button them over his seat."

The most difficult item of attire for the rural recruit to ad-

HALF AMERICAN, ALL JAPANESE

Captain Ryo Kurusu, a test pilot in the Japanese Army Air Force, disproved the notion that a son of two cultures can never be at home in either. He was thoroughly Japanese and intensely patriotic—despite the fact that his mother was American. His father, the distinguished diplomat Saburo Kurusu, had negotiated for peace in the United States before the outbreak of war.

Although the Kurusus gave their two daughters Western educations, they decided that Ryo should attend only Japanese schools. In the 1930s, while the family lived in a succession of European capitals, the boy went to technical school in Japan, studying engineering and, later, aircraft

design. After graduation, he joined the Army Air Force.

Throughout the War, Ryo chafed under the Army's slow, academic method of developing new warplanes. As a test pilot, he devoted every minute of his flying time to the creation of a fighter plane capable of challenging the American B-29. But on February 16, 1945, Ryo's work was cut short. Flying alone, he intercepted 30 U.S. carrier-based planes and shot down one of them before the others recovered and drove him off. Mortally wounded, his plane badly damaged, Ryo miraculously made it back to base and gave a full report of the engagement before he died.

Ambassador Kurusu and his American wife Alice, who spoke fluent Japanese, hoped their son might one day visit the United States.

An outspoken test pilot, Captain Ryo Kurusu frequently praised the design superiority of warplanes manufactured by the Americans.

just to was the Army's hobnailed boots. On the farm, the young men had worn *waraji* (straw sandals) or rubber-soled slippers, which separated the big toe from the other toes with a strap or secured it in an individual compartment. It took the country boys many painful days to get used to their confining boots.

The diet of the recruit was spartan at best, though it looked good at the start. "On the first day of my enlistment, we were given a special treat of glutinous rice cooked with red beans," said a former Yokohama shipyard worker. "But to our feast our superior officer added the comment: 'That's the last fine food you're going to get. Things are not going to be soft from now on.'" Afterward, a common breakfast for soldiers and sailors was cold rice and pickles and a cup of cold tea, all eaten in a great hurry so the men could return to their military duties. Lunch might consist of rice with a little meat or fish; supper was often no more than a bowl of soup with a little rice and vegetables.

The combat training of the recruit stressed stamina and ferocity. Since the great majority of the recruits would become infantrymen, all of them were subjected to endurance marches of 20 to 30 miles a day, with only a few brief breaks for rest or a meal. It was common practice for officers to order the men into a full run just as they neared complete exhaustion. Besides building up the recruit's endurance, this was supposed to prove to every man that he could do far more than he believed possible.

In at least one instance a commanding officer used an endurance march to underscore another vital point—that every soldier must obey orders without question, whatever the circumstances. As this officer led his men in a summer training exercise on the flanks of Mount Fuji, he forbade them to drink from their canteens without permission. He never gave permission, and no one disobeyed the order. Twenty men dropped from heat exhaustion; five of them died.

In addition to forced marches and war games, the recruits spent hours in small-arms training and bayonet drill. Wrestling classes were popular, though some instructors used a cruel technique to teach the recruits tenacity and aggressiveness. Saburo Sakai, who became a great naval air ace, later wrote of his pilot-training class in wrestling: "The instructor selected at random two students from the group and ordered them to wrestle. The victor of this clash was al-lowed to leave the wrestling mat. His opponent had no such luck. So long as he continued to lose, he remained on the mat, tiring with every bout.

"If necessary, he was forced to wrestle every one of the other 69 students in his class. If, at the end of 69 consecutive wrestling bouts, he was able to stand, he was considered fit—but only for one more day. The next day he again took on the first wrestling opponent and continued until he either emerged a victor or was expelled from the class."

Close attention was paid to the recruit's spiritual and psychological training. The Imperial Rescript to Soldiers and Sailors was read to the trainees on numerous occasions. Frequently, the men were roused from their cots in the middle of the night and marched to a shrine. They also were repeatedly indoctrinated with tenets that had descended from the samurai—for example, that they could defeat the enemy only if they put aside caution and concern for their own lives.

Time and again they were told to fight to the death or to commit suicide to avoid capture. The death of a Major Noboro Kuga was held up as a model of honor to all recruits. Kuga, a former schoolteacher, had been found unconscious by a Chinese soldier at the Battle of Shanghai in 1932. By a strange coincidence, the soldier had been a student of Kuga's in Japan, and he solicitously carried Kuga back to the Chinese lines and nursed him back to health. When Kuga recovered, he was released and allowed to return to his own forces. Because he had been taken prisoner, Kuga knew that he would face a court-martial, and that he probably would be acquitted because circumstances had made it impossible for him to commit suicide before he was captured. Nevertheless, Kuga felt disgraced. Returning to the place where he had been captured, he committed seppuku.

The failure of an officer to commit suicide to avoid capture was considered a breach of faith with his ancestors, his family, his comrades and his Emperor. This thought was so deep-seated that the Japanese officer found it shocking even to think of avoiding seppuku. One exception was Ensign Kazuo Sakamaki, the only survivor of the five minisubmarines that had vainly attacked Pearl Harbor in 1941. At first, Sakamaki was distraught that he had survived, but then he decided to go on living despite the shame. The moment of decision was, he later wrote, "like a sudden stab in my chest by a sharp knife. It was a stab against me, but it was more than that. It was a powerful hammer blow against the heart of my whole past, the past that represented the entire history and culture of Japan."

From the first day of training to the last, discipline was rigorously enforced, even for a recruit's slightest mistake or shortcoming. Pilot candidate Saburo Sakai recalled that a petty officer had punished him several times for minor offenses. " 'Stand to the wall. Bend down, Recruit Sakai,' he would order. 'I am doing this to you not because I hate you, but because I like you and want to make you a good seaman. Bend down!' "

With that, Sakai wrote, the petty officer would hit him as hard as he could across the backside with a large wooden club. "At times, I counted up to 40 crashing impacts on my buttocks. Often I fainted with pain. A lapse into unconsciousness constituted no escape, however. The petty officer simply hurled a bucket of cold water over my prostrate form and bellowed for me to resume position, whereupon he continued his 'discipline' until satisfied I would mend the error of my ways."

Each time a recruit was beaten for whatever cause, every other man in his company would be struck once by the petty officer or senior sergeant. And the recruits were expected to submit to their punishment stoically. "We were never allowed the indulgence of even a single satisfying groan in our misery," Sakai wrote. "Let one man moan in pain or anguish because of his 'paternalistic discipline' and to a man every recruit in the outfit would be kicked or dragged from his cot to receive the full course."

Once the recruit had completed his training, his lot improved. The beatings abated—he was now considered a man, not a thing. Nevertheless, arduous work kept him busy from dawn until late evening. A typical day began at 5:30 a.m. By 7 o'clock, the soldier was expected to have made his bed, helped clean the barracks, prepared for inspection and meditated on the soldierly virtues of the imperial rescript. A 10-minute breakfast at 7 a.m. was followed by five hours of drill and study. After a brief lunch at 12:10 p.m. came more studying and (if all chores had been done) a rest period from 4:10 until dinner at 5:30 p.m. After dinner came more work and study until lights out at 10 p.m.

The enlisted man normally had Sunday off, but he lacked the funds to venture far from his base. A private was paid the equivalent of $1.26 a month, which bought practically nothing. In any case, soldiers were expected to save most of their money. It was considered bad form—and very unlike a samurai—for a soldier or officer (lieutenants were paid $16.10 a month) who had money to spend too much of it at the company canteen indulging in cigarettes, candy, noodles, beer or sake.

Japanese officers had more in common with their men than the shared experience of a grueling daily regimen. Most of the officers came from the lower-middle class, and were socially not far removed from the farming and laboring backgrounds of their men. Whereas many of the recruits had ended their academic schooling in their early teens in order to work or learn a trade, however, most of the officers had gone on to the *yonen gakko*—the military preparatory schools. Although male graduates of all primary schools were eligible to take a national examination for entrance into the military schools, at the beginning of the War only one boy in about 60 passed the test. Later, as the need for officers increased, the entrance standards were relaxed.

After graduating from military school, Japan's future officers attended the Shikan Gakko in Tokyo, the Japanese equivalent of West Point, where a three-year curriculum

Tetsuji Kawakami, popular first baseman for the Tokyo Giants baseball team, scores a run during a game in 1940. Kawakami and many other players were drafted—some in mid-game. The stadium announcer would simply say, "Please return to your home for an official task."

was taught. The first course, lasting a year and a half during the War, was also open to graduates of the civilian middle schools who passed a tough entrance examination.

Men who took the first course graduated as sergeants. Those who completed the second, or senior, course received commissions as imperial officers. The academy's curriculum consisted almost entirely of military subjects: drill, tactics, horsemanship, fencing and marksmanship. The students learned nothing of political science, international relations or economics. These subjects were taught, however, at the Naval equivalent of the Shikan Gakko, the Imperial Naval Academy at Etajima near Hiroshima.

Not surprisingly, the Army's narrow curriculum produced officers who did poorly in managing their unit's budgets and in dealing with the people of occupied countries. The typical junior Army officer was ambitious, unsophisticated and utterly convinced that the Japanese spirit would prevail against any odds. Under the command of such men, thousands of soldiers would go to their deaths trying to match rifle bullets and bayonets in futile attacks against machine guns and artillery shells.

No family knew when its serviceman left the home islands or where he was bound—he simply disappeared. In time, a letter or letters might arrive from Borneo, the Philippines, the Marianas—though of course no good soldier would reveal his whereabouts. Some men wrote of their daily routine. Many letters spoke conventionally of the great honor of serving the Emperor, but others were highly personal and surprisingly frank.

Tokuo Nakamura wrote to his parents that he would not forget the hardships they had gone through to bring him up and regretted that he had lacked the filial piety to return their love in full measure. He said that the War was a tragedy and quoted a famous writer, Ryunosuke Akutagawa: " 'The beginning of tragedy is that parents have children and children have parents.' That is true. Blessings on you both." Nakamura was last seen in the Philippines in June 1944; he was 25 years old.

Man'nosuke Seda wrote to his mother and father: "I regret that I have been an atheist since my college days, now that I am wandering between life and death. It's not a question of what will happen to me after I die. I just feel that I'm missing something I can depend on. Now I understand the faith you both have. Please send me any book on religion. I just want to have peace of mind, even if it's temporary." Seda died in action in the Philippines in March of 1945, at the age of 21.

Airman Hachiro Sasaki wrote that a friend had argued, "dying in action for something that is not your own mission is just temporary heroism and is stupid." But Sasaki did not agree with his friend; thinking he had enjoyed a good life, he believed that "I have the happy duty to devote myself to my country." He died in the air over Okinawa in April 1945. He was 23.

A soldier named Kinpei Matsuoka wrote, "I care for my life, but that's not the only thing in this world." All of his schoolmates would sacrifice their lives to secure Japan's place in Asia, he said, and "I'm going to die believing in that." But he added a note of doubt: "What if it doesn't

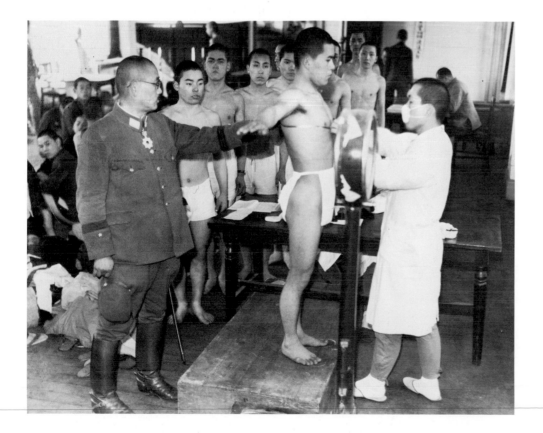

Teen-age draftees take a preinduction physical under the scrutiny of an Army officer in 1944. To qualify for the armed forces, a man had to stand at least 4 feet 10½ inches, weigh at least 103 pounds and have a chest measurement more than half his height.

work out that way?'' Matsuoka was killed in action in Burma in 1945, at the age of 22.

Another soldier, Shin Hasegawa, wrote that the thought of killing or being killed was repulsive. He asked for a transfer to the air corps: "Eventually I may kill people but at least I won't have to do it with my own hands." Lamenting that "there is no issue of justice in this War, just the explosion of hatred among races," Hasegawa concluded that "human beings everywhere are relatives of the apes." He was 23 when he died in aerial combat over Okinawa in 1945.

For many families, either no letter arrived or the mail suddenly stopped. There was a long, frightening silence and the

Uniformed middle-school students watch as recently drafted college students (foreground) march in review during a massive send-off held at Tokyo's Meiji Stadium in October 1943. Some 650 of the college recruits who took part in the rally would die as Kamikaze pilots.

family felt a deep sense of estrangement from its distant warrior. Then the silence would be broken by the arrival of a messenger who recited the official words of sympathy: "Please accept this notice comforted by the knowledge that your son died for His Imperial Majesty, the Emperor. We express our deepest condolences to the soul of a hero."

If the family members were thoroughly grounded in the Way of the Warrior, those few words were a comfort. They believed that the soul of the fallen soldier, at the very instant of death, had been transported to Tokyo's Yasukuni Shrine. There, amid the cherry trees of Kudan Hill, the name of the dead warrior was inscribed on giant black-and-gold tablets. Said a Japanese writer about a prayer ceremony at Yasukuni: "The soldiers become deities to guard the Empire. They are no longer human. As they are enshrined at Yasukuni, they retain no rank or other distinction. Generals and privates are alike. They are the pillars of the nation and because of that they are worshipped by the Emperor and the entire population."

Though Japanese women accepted the solace of Yasukuni and were publicly stoic about their loss, they were nonetheless grief-stricken at the death of a loved one, and at times their composure cracked. The mother of a Navy pilot who had just been reported dead showed no sign of grief when she visited her son's former schoolteacher, Takaaki Aikawa. "She suddenly walked into my garden," wrote Aikawa. "Seeing her bright smile, I thought she had good news. Standing on the dug-up ground, she began talking in an ordinary way about the weather, rationing and communications. Suddenly, she blurted out, 'My boy had the honor of dying for his country.'

"I could not say anything, struck dumb by her sudden words. I gazed at her face, which still had not lost its tranquillity. Then, with a glare flashing in her eyes she said, 'Mr. Aikawa, you think my boy shot down one enemy plane at least, don't you?' The hard glare had no sooner come than it was gone, and she was once again the gentle Japanese mother with a smile, that famous smile that never leaves the lips, even at the death of a loved one."

As she turned to leave his garden, said Aikawa, "I saw her take out a small handkerchief. She seemed to be wiping her forehead, but I knew she was weeping, weeping in her heart, clenching her teeth very hard while still holding that masklike smile."

Sometime after a family learned of the death of a loved one in battle, his ashes would be returned home. It became commonplace all over Japan to see soldiers carrying the ashes of comrades home in small, white wood boxes like the one in which the ashes of Admiral Yamamoto had been placed in 1943.

Upon boarding or leaving a train or boat, the bearer wore a rough white cloth about his neck to support the box. If the soldier had been traveling in a second-class compartment, he always made a point of leaving from the first-class section to give added honor to the ashes.

When the ashes arrived, friends and neighbors of the dead man's family lined the streets to pay their respects. If the ashes of several men came back at the same time, there was a joint funeral. Families placed pictures of the slain soldiers, draped with black ribbon, on the altar of the local Buddhist temple, and set before them offerings of fruit, rice cakes and burning incense. When the ashes were interred in a Shinto ceremony, each dead man was said to have joined the demigods of Japanese classic myth.

As Japan's military fortunes declined, the Army and Navy found it increasingly difficult to return the ashes of servicemen who had been killed in action. Hiroshi Fujino, the head of a neighborhood association in Tokyo, recalled having to read a depressing statement to the members of his group: "Families of those soldiers going to active fronts are advised to save locks of hair or pieces of fingernails to guard against not having anything at all of the person of the honored dead."

A NATION OF SAMURAI

The 12th Century warrior Minamoto Yoshitsune (right)—one of the greatest samurai—displays his swordsmanship against his legendary foe, the priest Benkai.

ANCIENT INSPIRATION FOR A MODERN WARRIOR

Bayonet-tipped rifles at the ready, camouflaged Japanese soldiers await mock combat in prewar maneuvers between "East" and "West" armies.

In the skies over the Yangtze River in China on October 3, 1939, fighter pilot Saburo Sakai flew alone into a hail of fire from 12 enemy bombers; he shot down one of them and escaped unharmed. Sakai, who was to become one of Japan's most honored aviators in World War II, had not been daunted by the impossible odds. "There was no delaying my attack," he wrote of the episode. "I had been raised in the samurai tradition, and there was no thought other than to wreak all the damage I could."

That samurai tradition, the legacy of ancient Japan's sword-wielding warrior class, flamed anew in wartime Japan. Like airman Sakai, millions of Japanese were guided by the age-old samurai tenets: raw courage, unstinting obedience and contempt for death.

Such virtues were instilled at an early age. Japanese schoolboys learned "samurai spirit" through bruising calisthenics, sometimes performed bare-chested in the snow, and home discipline that included frequent thrashings and bracing cold baths.

As part of their training, young recruits in the Japanese Army each night recited a maxim that echoed an old samurai proverb: "Duty is heavier than a mountain, while death is lighter than a feather." In combat, the ingrained acceptance of pain and death led the Japanese soldier to shun safety measures as cowardly. Pilots frequently went without parachutes. Combat units often included no medics. And soldiers were duty-bound to choose death over capture. Thus when faced with inevitable defeat, soldiers by the thousands staged suicidal charges and their commanding officers committed seppuku, or ritual suicide. In doing so, they followed the advice of a 17th Century samurai manual: "To die having failed is not a shameful thing."

Such behavior was incomprehensible to Japan's Western enemies, but the ferocity of the Japanese soldier at times drew their grudging praise. "We talk a lot about fighting to the last man and the last round," said British Field Marshal Viscount William J. Slim, "but only the Japanese soldier actually does it."

In this 19th Century wood block, a victorious samurai bloodied by arrows reins in his mount over his dead and wounded enemies.

Swordsmith Sanjo-kokaji Munechika raises a burly arm to forge a blade called Kogitsune Maru—Little Fox. The fox spirit, assuming the form of a lad, looks over Munechika's shoulder to imbue the blade with his essence.

A court sword (below) of ancient style boasts a sharkskin hilt, enamel studs, gilt sword mounts and a lacquered scabbard decorated with inlaid mother-of-pearl birds. A fierce but delicately engraved dragon (inset) creeps toward the point of a gleaming blade that probably was forged in the early 1800s.

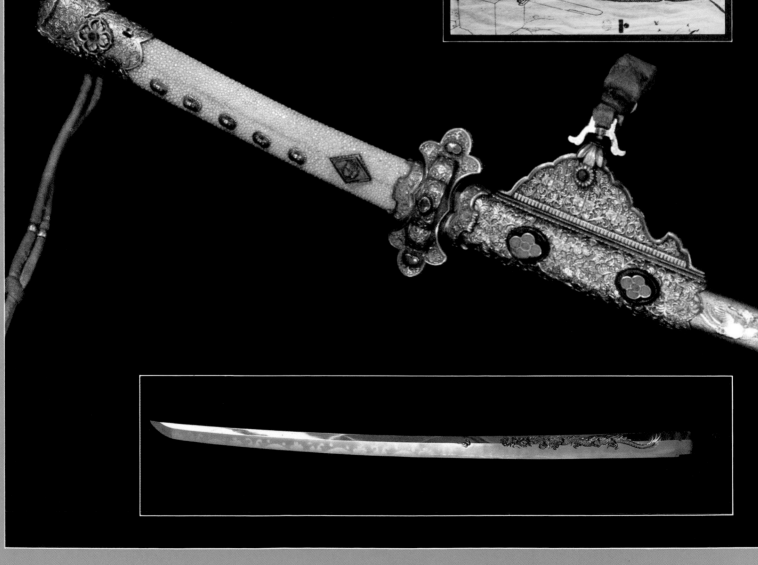

Sword drawn, a Japanese officer leads his men against the Chinese. Officers were quick to use their swords and were prone to lead samurai-like charges.

THE LONG SWORD-- "SOUL OF THE SAMURAI"

The long sword was the samurai's weapon *par excellence*. Its gracefully curved blade —an unrivaled cutting edge that could cleave bone and even steel—took months to shape. But the final product, as the emblem of the samurai class, was worth the effort and expense. It was a work of art, and the warrior's most prized possession.

The samurai spent years practicing *kendo*, or the Way of the Sword. *Kendo*, as it was taught by the great 17th Century sword fighter Miyamoto Musashi, aimed far beyond skill with the weapon itself: "To master the long sword," wrote Musa-shi, "is to govern the world and oneself."

Samurai swords were no less important to the modern Army—at least symbolically. Officers and Kamikaze pilots wore them, and many of these men put their families deep into debt to buy the best and oldest swords they could find. The swords served as visible reminders of Japan's glorious history—and of the warrior's duty. Even the lowliest soldier, though denied a sword himself, was expected to share in the mystique: "The samurai regarded his sword as his soul," an officer told recruits, "and so must the soldier regard his rifle."

The 47 ronin swarm over Lord Kira's stronghold on the night of December 14, 1703, to achieve their long-sought revenge for the death of their lord.

THE ENDURING LEGACY OF THE 47 RONIN

"Wherever we may be," declared an old samurai text, "our duty is to guard the interest of our lord." That and other lessons of the samurai code were fixed in the Japanese memory by a riveting saga of the 18th Century.

According to legend, in 1701 a provincial lord named Asano attacked the shogun's master of ceremonies, Lord Kira, for deliberately embarrassing Asano on a point of court etiquette. Kira survived, but Asano was ordered to commit seppuku because he had illegally drawn his sword in the shogun's palace. Upon Asano's death, 47 of his warriors—who became *ronin,* or masterless samurai—swore revenge.

To deceive Kira, the 47 *ronin* pretended to abandon all sense of samurai honor. They engaged in brawls, slept drunk in the streets and even let their swords rust. After two years of shameless dissipation, on a snowy, moonlit night in December, they successfully attacked Kira's mansion and demanded that Kira too commit seppuku. When he refused, they beheaded him (using the short sword with which Asano had killed himself) and carried his head to Asano's grave.

Their vengeance now complete, the *ronin* surrendered and awaited judgment. They had performed their single-minded duty in full knowledge that it might cost them their lives. In unhesitating submission to their inevitable sentence, they all committed seppuku.

The *ronin* were buried beside their lord in tombs that instantly became a shrine. Their story galvanized the nation, inspiring a kabuki play and, later, everything from puppet shows to motion pictures.

They also inspired imitators. The bravery and selflessness of the *ronin,* according to an elementary-school reader that was used during the War, were "to be regarded as an example for ages eternal." It was an example that many a Japanese soldier, laden with dynamite, would follow on the field of combat.

Tokyo schoolboys bow before a shrine honoring the "Three Human Bombs": soldiers who in 1932 reportedly breached Shanghai's defenses by blowing themselves up with a torpedo-like land mine. "We thought of these men," said a teacher, "as the epitome of courage and devotion to one's country."

In a 19th Century representative woodcut, women armed with traditional long-handled swords (right) stand their ground against a charge by mounted government troops toward the end of a samurai revolt in 1877.

A Japanese Army officer trains housewives to fight with bamboo spears in anticipation of a last-ditch defense of the home islands in 1945.

"TO MATCH OUR FLESH AGAINST THEIR STEEL"

It was a great honor to be the first warrior to engage the enemy in combat: A samurai proudly chanted his name and ancestry while leading an attack. It was also a samurai's inescapable duty to fight to the bitter end, even in the face of defeat.

That duty was shouldered in modern Japan by thousands of young men, many of them untrained, who volunteered for Kamikaze missions near the end of the War. In the samurai tradition, they faced death unflinchingly. "If you start out on a mission with the idea of coming back," a suicide pilot said, "you won't be able to carry it out with 100 per cent efficiency."

Many civilians shared both the samurai's determination to fight on and the Kamikaze pilot's resolve to die "a beautiful death." One woman slit her throat when her husband left for the front. "Please do not worry about your home," she wrote, "for there is no longer anything to make you worry. Powerless as I am, I am doing what little I can so you and your men may fight with heart and soul for the country."

Other Japanese women emulated the wives of ancient samurai and learned to fight with spears, confidently determined —if an Allied invasion came—"to match our training against their numbers and our flesh against their steel."

140

A COUNTRY TOWN AT WAR

Draftees escorted by soldiers and local veterans march past a throng of cheering citizens of Chichibu on the way to the mountain town's railway station.

RITUAL AND ROUTINE IN WARTIME CHICHIBU

Cupped high in the mountains 60 miles northwest of Tokyo, the town of Chichibu was one of a thousand quiet backwaters feeding the tide of conquest that surged outward from Japan during the War. For 50 years Chichibu and its outlying villages had provided tough peasant fighters for the expeditionary forces that had made Japan an imperial power. Now men of the district streamed from the mountain hamlets in even greater numbers, marching down Chichibu's unpaved main street to the trains that would take them to training camps or to ships bound for the battlefronts.

Chichibu sacrificed more than its young men to the War. By 1942 most of the local mills that produced luxurious silks had been converted to the manufacture of blankets for troops, and the young women workers were compelled by the government to labor at their looms and sewing machines for poverty wages. The remaining mills had been closed down, and the employees had to seek work outside Chichibu. Even as its economy collapsed, the town swelled with unemployed refugees from the overcrowded, stringently rationed cities.

The townspeople—old residents and newcomers, children, mothers and the elderly—worked in unison to maintain the life of Chichibu and to contribute to their country's war effort. They spent arduous days tilling and extending patches of precious farmland to fill the government's demands for rice and wheat. They gathered wood and made charcoal and pried iron ore from skimpy deposits in the mountains. The strongest among them hauled limestone chunks from quarries to the local cement factory.

Their hard-won achievements did not go unrecorded. From early 1942 until the summer of 1943, a visual account of life in the town was compiled by an enterprising local photographer named Buko Shimizu. Appointed by the Photographers' Patriotic Association to provide morale-boosting family portraits for the people of the town and the hamlets around it, young Shimizu used part of his film to capture the story of Chichibu itself: the rituals and the often poignant routines of a country town at war.

Chichibu's geisha set out to gather wood. Until 1942 these well-bred women catered at parties for mill managers, silk buyers and local gentry.

Accompanied by a color guard, veterans of previous wars lead an assembly ot Chichibu residents in prayers for victory in·front of the town's Shinto shrine.

FOR ONE AND ALL, SWEAT AND SACRIFICE

The War made huge demands on Chichibu. Local school children, their numbers swollen by transfers from the city, took over most of the agricultural work when the area's farmers were drafted. As the national labor pool dwindled and the demand for food and raw materials increased, Chichibu's students had to abandon their studies and devote all their time to working in the fields and rice paddies.

Monks and priests of the numerous local Buddhist temples and priests of the Shinto shrines were not exempt from the war effort, either. They had to curtail their spiritual pursuits and go to work, like the children, tilling the soil and raising crops.

The women of the town contributed in a number of ways. The Chichibu mothers' club—renamed the Women's Defense Association—raised and skinned rabbits to provide fur linings for the uniforms of soldiers stationed in Manchuria. And Chichibu's geisha, who in their professional duties had rarely lifted anything heavier than a teapot, found themselves toting loads of kindling over mountain trails—work that horses had done before the War.

High-school girls harvest wheat in a schoolyard once used for volleyball.

146

Two youngsters with an ox plow a rice paddy for planting while their schoolmates thrust rows of rice shoots into the mud of previously prepared ground.

Spicing his lecture with humor, an old farmer offers pointers on rabbit-raising to a class of smiling young mothers and their children.

A lumberjack prepares to top a cypress in a government project that stripped Chichibu of most of its precious, ancient groves.

148

Aged woodcutters help women of the Chichibu geisha association load firewood they have collected into barrel-shaped containers for transport into town.

大東京帝國大學

翼賛政

醫學徒報國隊

A banner advertising a visit by medical students from Tokyo draws mothers and children from all over the Chichibu area for checkups and treatment.

A horse-drawn wagon on rails brings medical students to a hamlet.

Carried by her son, an ailing woman descends a path to Chichibu.

MEDICAL HELP FOR A DOCTORLESS TOWN

A visit from outsiders in the summer of 1942 stirred a flurry of excitement in isolated Chichibu. Since early in the War, when the town's last physician was drafted, the town had gone without professional medical care. Now help arrived—in the form of medical students from Tokyo Imperial University. Such roving teams of student doctors were the best that wartime Japan could do for its rural communities, 3,650 of which had no resident physician.

At Chichibu, the medical students treated all comers but paid special attention to the children, giving them diphtheria and smallpox inoculations, carefully checking their height, weight and general condition. Here, as in other rural towns, they found that about 20 per cent of the children less than two years old were underweight and suffering from dietary deficiencies.

"Do you get enough to eat?" the students asked the older children. Only one in 10 answered yes.

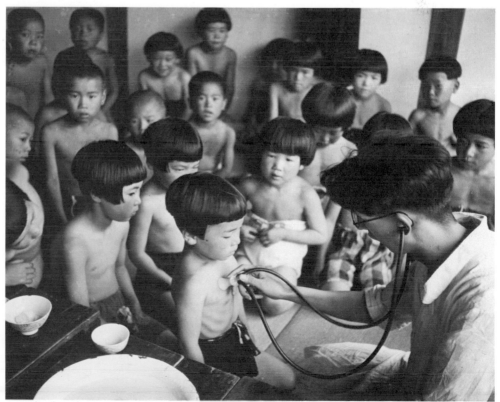

A medical student examines local preschoolers. During the War most children lost several pounds.

Preceded by a flag-bearer, a boy carrying his father's memorial tablet leads a funeral procession into Chichibu's main square. His relatives follow a soldier who carries the ashes.

THE RETURN OF FALLEN HEROES

The parades in Chichibu late in the War were a far cry from the early ones, when all Chichibu had turned out to cheer recruits and to celebrate victories. More and more the parades were silent, somber funeral processions. At mass funeral ceremonies, flags arrayed before the town hall were dipped to honor the dead. Inside, identical boxes filled with ashes sat on Buddhist altars, along with portraits of husbands and sons killed in action.

"The young men we had seen off at the shrines or at the station returned as the ashes of fallen heroes," recalled photographer Buko Shimizu, "and I, as a young man, began to realize that I too might be a short distance from death." Shimizu would survive the War. But he was called up in July 1943, and for the last time he clicked his shutter on the home-front warriors of Chichibu.

On an altar in Chichibu's town hall, incense burners bearing Buddhist swastikas are lined up beneath

photographs of the town's war dead and beribboned boxes containing their cremated remains. Above each box, a tablet displays the name of the deceased.

5

One of Tokyo's periodic air-raid drills was drawing to a close during the lunch hour on April 18, 1942, when a flight of 16 twin-engined aircraft approached the city from the north. Seventeen-year-old Minoru Iida, a student at a commercial high school, watched the lead plane roar low over his house. He saw blazoned on its wings an unfamiliar white-star insignia, and then black cylinders came tumbling from the plane's belly. This was no drill, Minoru realized with horror; these bombs were real. "Enemy plane!" he shouted. "It's an air raid!"

A small metal cylinder clattered onto the tile roof of the Iida family's home and lodged in the eaves. It was a six-pound incendiary bomb, much like the one described in the air-raid training classes that a member from every Tokyo household was obliged to attend. Grabbing a bucket of sand from his house, as he had been taught, Minoru smothered the sputtering bomb. Two more incendiaries had landed in the street nearby, and he and another youth doused those with sand-filled paper bags.

The air raid, Japan's first, ended about an hour later and the damage proved to be negligible: Only a few dozen houses were destroyed and 12 people were killed. But in almost every other respect, the results of the attack were alarming. The people of Tokyo, who had believed in spite of their drills that they would never see an air raid, were so surprised and excited by the spectacle that they forgot about their air-defense duties and gathered in the streets or climbed on rooftops to watch the show. Only children—and not many of them—sought safety in the shelters.

The air-raid shelters themselves—insufficient in number and mostly shallow affairs—offered occupants little protection from high-explosive bombs that landed anywhere close to them. But government propaganda minimized the danger: "The number of victims of the blast effect was not as great as reported. Those who were felled by direct hits were just unlucky."

Most disturbing of all, the success of Minoru Iida and others in extinguishing the American fire bombs convinced the authorities that, as a government release asserted, "We have nothing to fear from incendiary bombs."

Thoughtful people did not believe that story. They knew that Tokyo was an immense tinderbox; around its concrete office buildings and cinder-block factories sprawled more

A SPRINGTIME OF FIRE

than 200 square miles of wood-and-paper houses, most of them spaced only inches apart. The houses had wooden floors covered with thick straw mats, thin wood-and-plaster outer walls, and translucent paper for doors, windows and lamps. The citizens cooked with charcoal or with gas piped from shallow mains. For light they used kerosene lamps or electricity from low-strung power lines.

A stray spark was a terrible hazard in Tokyo—indeed in all of Japan's wood-and-paper cities. Great blazes had often started when the winds of late winter scattered charcoal cooking fires or blew down paper lanterns. Three times in the 1920s and 1930s, earthquakes had touched off citywide conflagrations in Tokyo and Yokohama. On September 1, 1923, fires started by a quake consumed half of Tokyo and incinerated nearly 100,000 people.

Tokyo was woefully ill-equipped to fight a great fire. Its municipal fire department had too little gear, and much of what it had was either antiquated or substandard; besides, the drafting of maintenance men into military service had left at least 20 per cent of the fire trucks constantly out of commission, awaiting repair. The firemen, commanded by officials who were mainly concerned with military discipline, spent more time in close-order drill than they did in training to fight fires.

Ultimately, Japan's cities were indefensible against large-scale air attack with incendiaries. The only hope was to keep enemy bombers beyond striking distance, and the Japanese government remained confident of doing so. This first raid apparently had come from an American aircraft carrier (it was, in fact, Lieut. Colonel James H. Doolittle's raid from the carrier *Hornet*), for Japanese air attacks on General Douglas MacArthur's air force in the Philippines in December 1941 had destroyed the enemy's last land-based bombers within range of Japan. And plans were already afoot to wipe out the carriers and other remnants of the U.S. Pacific Fleet in a single naval battle.

That great sea battle, fought near Midway Island eight weeks later, failed to destroy the U.S. fleet. Nevertheless, the Doolittle raid would not be repeated. The United States was building a new class of bomber, the B-29, with a very long range, and until it was deployed there were no air raids, restoring what little confidence the Japanese home front had lost during the pinprick attack of April 1942. No one dreamed that before the War was over Japan would suffer more losses of life and property from conventional air raids than any other nation.

In the immediate aftermath of the Doolittle strike, Prime Minister Tojo's government did press for improved air-raid precautions by what had always been the nation's main line of defense against fire: individual citizens, organized by their neighborhood associations. Through stepped-up inspections of the 10 to 12 houses under its jurisdiction, each of the million-odd neighborhood associations saw to it that every home had sand, tanks of water, buckets, shovels and brooms, and that residents knew how to use them against incendiary bombs. The associations led bucket-brigade drills and enforced blackout regulations. All citizens were required to take an "air-defense oath of certain victory," in which they vowed to "refrain from selfish conduct" and to band together to defend the neighborhood. After 1943, essential workers were forbidden by a new national air-defense law to leave the cities during air raids.

Prodded by the neighborhood associations and by government exhortation, the citizens of Tokyo and other cities dug family air-raid shelters in their gardens, grumbling at the effort. As soon as they had planked over the shallow holes, they mounded dirt on the roofs and planted flowers and vegetables to beautify the ugly protuberances.

During practice blackouts, the roof of the dugout usually became a roost instead of a shelter. Nobody cared to descend into the dank pits, which soon filled with ground water, and in any case somebody was required to stay above ground to watch for incendiaries and summon help to smother them, or to man bucket brigades if the fire spread.

The municipal government ordered ditches dug in commercial centers for those caught in a raid while out shopping. Almost at once the new shelters caused casualties and complaints; people stumbled into the ditches during blackouts or on their way home from neighborhood bars, and suffered broken limbs and cracked skulls. Similarly, people grumbled about the huge vats that were set up at regular intervals to store water for fire fighting; the stagnant water bred mosquitoes.

Before long, the shock of the Doolittle raid faded. The authorities had to keep sloganeering at a high pitch to stifle grumbling and maintain training discipline. The United States had won steppingstone victories in New Guinea and the Solomon and Gilbert Islands before the government could revive home-front interest in air-raid precautions. The director of Tokyo's Ueno Park Zoo, on his own authority, ordered the lions and other dangerous animals destroyed; he did not want terrified predators roaming loose if bombs damaged the zoo. The Diet buildings were camouflaged with nets. The first serious thought was given in Tokyo to evacuating residents—vital government office workers had priority on the list—but the plans were not published.

Late in 1943 the Home Ministry established a central air-defense headquarters in Tokyo. It ordered that firebreaks be cut through the capital, and lines of buildings were designated for demolition. The residents and owners of the condemned buildings were told they would have to find replacements on their own, and eventually 20,000 displaced persons—with some government help—crowded in with friends, homesteaded in abandoned buildings or picked up and moved in with relatives in the country.

In the summer of 1944, the home front received two mighty scares. First, the Americans sent their huge new B-29 Superfortresses into action. These planes, which flew farther and faster and carried more explosive tonnage than any other bomber in the U.S. arsenal, mounted their first attack on June 16. Striking from bases in China at the closest of the home islands, Kyushu, they hit the Yawata steel mill and the Kokura industrial complex. But the logistical difficulties of bombing from bases in central China were immense, and the U.S. sorties against Japan were relatively few. Over the next five months, the B-29s staged nine scattered and sporadic attacks on Kyushu's other industrial plants, airfields and Naval bases.

To the great relief of the Japanese, the attacks were not particularly destructive. The B-29s in China were operating at the outer limits of their 3,500-mile range, the crews had not yet mastered the new aircraft, and their high-explosive bombs were for the most part poorly aimed. Professional and volunteer fire fighters dealt with the damage matter-of-factly, and fires set by misdirected bombs in residential areas were put out by trained local residents. Meanwhile, and far more dangerous, in June U.S. forces invaded Saipan and Tinian in Japan's own southern sea, just 1,300 miles

south of Tokyo. Even before the Marianas were secured, the Americans went to work turning Saipan and Tinian into giant air bases for hundreds of Superforts.

The piercing of Japan's inner defensive ring had immediate political consequences in Tokyo. It strengthened the hand of a small group of thoughtful Japanese leaders—led by elder statesmen and Navy men—who wanted to negotiate an end to the War. Among them were three former Prime Ministers: Admiral Keisuke Okada, who had escaped the swords of Army mutineers in 1936, Prince Fumimaro Konoe, the well-meaning aristocrat who had been manipulated by the militarists in their rise to power in the late 1930s, and Admiral Mitsumasa Yonai, who had opposed Japan's alliance with Germany and who had doubted his nation's ability to wage war against America and Britain.

These men had long since agreed that the first step toward peace was to obtain General Tojo's resignation as Prime Minister, a task they went about in true Japanese fashion. For a year they worked carefully and circuitously in order not to arouse resentment or dissension. Okada said later that "since it was impossible to launch an open movement to overthrow the Cabinet in the wartime situation, it would be best for Tojo to leave his post without losing face."

In February the elder statesmen met with Tojo and ac-

A Tokyo girl stands ready for air-raid drill in March 1944. She wears thick trousers, a long-sleeved blouse and a padded hood for protection against flames and falling debris, and a towel over her belt for bandaging injuries. Sewed to her vest is a tag bearing her name and school.

cused him of not telling the truth about Japan's chances in the War. Afterward, Konoe purposefully spread the word of the group's dissatisfaction with Tojo and was so effective that when Tojo appeared in the Diet, he was greeted with silence instead of the usual applause—a hint of trouble that he was quick to note.

Now Okada moved like a judo expert to turn the Prime Minister's strength against him. The Navy Minister, Admiral Shigetaro Shimada, was a close friend of Tojo's; under his leadership the Navy had been unable to counter the Army's dictation of national policy and the conduct of the War. But if this key official could be persuaded or pressured to resign, the Cabinet might fall.

Shimada, who was held in contempt by his fellow admirals for his subservience to Tojo, met separately with Okada and with Fleet Admiral Prince Fushimi, both of whom urged him to resign in the interests of the Navy and the country. Unmoved, Shimada advised Prince Fushimi to leave town for his own good, while Tojo called in Okada and warned him to desist or suffer "troublesome consequences." Then Tojo went to the Lord Keeper of the Privy Seal, Koichi Kido, the Emperor's closest adviser, to enlist support for strengthening the Cabinet. Kido had been instrumental in making Tojo Prime Minister in 1941, and Tojo was certain that he would put an end to Okada's seditious politicking.

Tojo got a rude shock, for Okada and Kido had been conferring for more than a year. Kido told Tojo that Shimada should retire, and that Tojo himself would have to surrender his post as chief of the Army general staff and admit some elder statesmen to the Cabinet. "Who says so?" shot back the Prime Minister. "These are the wishes of His Imperial Majesty," was the bland reply, confirmed by Tojo during an audience with the Emperor the next day. Desperately, Tojo tried to enlist another malleable admiral to replace Shimada and to find an inconspicuous Cabinet position for one of the elder statesmen. But again Okada was ahead of him with a counter to each maneuver.

The final blow came on July 17, 1944, when the elder statesmen, led by Konoe and Kido, drafted a statement for the Emperor calling for a united Cabinet, an oblique but clearly understood way of saying that Tojo should step down. The next day the Emperor quickly and gratefully endorsed the statement, and Tojo, realizing he had no support, resigned on July 18. But he was not disgraced and the nation was not split by a political fight. Tojo remained as an elder statesman and in fact continued to influence national policy through his Army commanders. The new Prime Minister, General Kuniaki Koiso, was not under Tojo's thumb, but he lacked the strength to take an independent course.

The new government was still struggling to organize itself when, on November 1, 1944, the first B-29 appeared over Tokyo. It came not to drop bombs but to photograph targets and test Tokyo's meager antiaircraft defenses. At midmonth came six more B-29s on a dry run; lunch-hour crowds stood out on the sidewalks to view the silvery craft, so high they looked like toys, so powerful their distant roar evoked awe, so beautiful they inspired grudging admiration.

Then, on the 24th of November, 94 B-29s soared over Tokyo's industrial outskirts. The people below did not take them seriously, even when they began dropping bombs. Reporter Masuo Kato observed that "air-raid discipline was extremely poor because so many residents wanted to see what was happening." Kato and his friends, oblivious to the antiaircraft shrapnel that filled the sky, dashed into the street without their helmets to watch. Eventually they were ordered into a shelter by the police, but not before they had seen a restaurant next to the Imperial Hotel go up in flames.

It was clear to all that this raid and others that soon followed were aimed at aircraft plants and military installations outside the city, and that the occasional hits on residential areas were unfortunate accidents. The high-flying B-29s did little damage even to their primary target, the Nakajima aircraft complex in the suburb of Musashino, and most of the bombs aimed at the docks and warehouses along Tokyo Bay fell wide of their mark. Occasionally a lightweight magnesium or phosphorous bomb bounced off a householder's roof or penetrated an upstairs ceiling. A bucket of sand, a wet mop or a water-soaked mat, used at once, would extinguish such an incendiary.

In fact, most Tokyo residents were more fascinated than frightened by the first B-29 raids. "We went through those early bombings in a spirit of excitement and suspense," journalist Kato recalled. "There was even a spirit of adventure, a sense of exultation in sharing the dangers of war even though bound to civilian existence."

Uniformed school children board a special evacuation train, identified by the sign at center, in Tokyo.

Led by their smiling teachers, school children arrive in the country, parading before a welcoming group of schoolmates who had been evacuated earlier.

In the summer of 1944, when American forces seized the Mariana Islands, which were within bomber range of Japan, about 400,000 school children were evacuated from Japanese cities to the countryside. From Tokyo alone, 250,000 children were shipped to 12 nearby prefectures.

Though the youngsters were relatively safe, their life in the country was hardly idyllic. Even there, classes often were interrupted by air-raid alerts. After school, the children were put to work gathering mountain herbs or growing vegetables to supplement their meager diet.

Not surprisingly, most of the city-bred youngsters had a difficult time adapting to their new environment. Fleas, lice and hunger were their constant companions. And they feared for the parents they had left behind. "You'd hear the bombs go off and see the sky turn half-red," one girl remembered. "I was always worried and homesick. There were times when I felt like walking home."

Grinning evacuees take turns scrubbing each other's backs and soaking in a communal bath.

Relocated children give thanks for a simple meal of thin soup, rice and beans. The lack of a balanced diet made malnutrition common among the evacuees.

It was a common attitude. People discerned patterns in the bombings, and they adjusted their lives to them. Daylight attacks usually came at lunchtime and lasted two to three hours. In November and December the raids on Tokyo happened to come only on dates divisible by three: the 24th, the 27th, the 30th, the 3rd, and so on. Housewives scheduled their shopping trips according to this timetable and stayed home between noon and 3 p.m. on those days. People joked about the B-29s' "regularly scheduled service" and speculated on what the pilots overhead might be having for lunch: "Some nice ham sandwiches, perhaps."

Night raids were less easy to adjust to, though people tried to go to bed early to get some sleep before the red-alert sirens sounded around 11:30 p.m. The night raiders—they were called "the honorable visitors"—had their own fascination. When a B-29 emerged from the layers of winter cloud and industrial haze and was caught in a searchlight beam, it was greeted with shouts of "There's Lord B!" by people standing watch on factory rooftops or sitting on porches or on the mounds covering their garden shelters. The searchlights, the bursts of antiaircraft fire, the fighter planes darting upward, even the glow of distant fires produced a riveting but dangerous nighttime spectacle.

The U.S. Army Air Forces was trying to knock out Japan's aircraft industry with precision bombing. In addition to the sprawling Nakajima complex at Musashino, near Tokyo, the big Mitsubishi aircraft plant in Nagoya was a frequent target, as were plants in Omura, Kobe and Osaka. But the bombing was far from precise, mostly because of the clouds that covered Japan throughout the winter, and the planes were hitting less than 20 per cent of their targets. On one overcast Saturday in January 1945, a formation of 15 B-29s attempted to bomb the Musashino plants, setting off the Tokyo air-raid sirens. Unable to see through Musashino's thick cloud cover, the bombardiers instead dumped their high-explosive loads on their alternate target, downtown Tokyo. They hit the city's Fifth Avenue, the Ginza, just as crowds of shoppers, hearing a mistaken all clear, emerged from the shelters. Hundreds died in a subway station that took a direct hit, hundreds more in theaters, in the streets and beneath the arches of elevated railways. The Musashino plants were untouched.

The B-29s kept on trying, with only modest success, to knock out the Musashino complex. Then on February 17, a single attack by U.S. Navy carrier planes did more damage than the half-dozen Superfort raids that had preceded it. The

Hellcats and Corsair fighter-bombers came in low and devastated the plants, knocking out much of the Musashino production line. It was a serious blow, for the pace of aircraft production had already fallen behind the loss rate.

Month after month, the effectiveness of the B-29s was seriously reduced by thick clouds and high winds that made precision bombing from high altitudes nearly impossible. The Americans tried a change in tactics: On February 25, B-29s pelted Tokyo with massed incendiaries, trying to burn out the workers' wooden houses along with the factories. The winds came to Tokyo's rescue. As each ungainly and unstable 500-pound cluster tumbled from the planes at 30,000 feet, the winds carried its many incendiaries into Tokyo Bay or across the countryside, or scattered them so widely that individual fires could be dealt with fairly easily.

But on March 9, the winds turned against the Japanese, with cataclysmic result. Though dawn that day brought Tokyo a soft, early-spring morning, a bit of gusty March wind picked up in the afternoon and became quite strong by evening. This time the people of Tokyo were alert in their flimsy houses, for such weather always intensified the danger of fire in the densely packed capital.

At 10:30 p.m., radio broadcasts warned that B-29s were approaching; the information had been relayed by watchers on the chain of islands that stretch south of Tokyo Bay to the Bonins. A little later the first air-raid sirens wailed.

Just before midnight the lead plane roared in low and fast from the east, dropping clusters of 70-pound napalm bombs that gushed streaks of flaming jelly wherever they hit. A second pathfinder crossed the track of the first at the Sumida River, completing a fiery X across the northeast quarter of the darkened city, a low-lying plain of factories, workshops and small houses sprawled on either side of the river.

Then, more than 250 B-29s thundered in at 10,000 feet or lower. The bombardiers, sighting on the fires already started, dumped clusters of oil and napalm canisters into the dark spots. Driven by a 28-mile-per-hour ground wind, each new burst flared outward and upward, whirling 100 feet in the air and snapping across alleys and firebreaks to find new fuel in structures of pine, paper, straw and bamboo. In the first 15 minutes great patches of the wooden city erupted into flame. The intensity of the fires whipped the

winds to 40 miles per hour and more. Now the conflagration was everywhere out of control.

Though encircled by flame, householders at first tried to carry out the fire drills they had practiced, pouncing on each bomb with water or sand, standing by to form communal bucket brigades and looking to the orders of policemen, fire fighters and the few trained rescue workers. If each household did its part, so the authorities had said, every neighborhood could provide its own protection and thus the entire city would be safeguarded. But no one had imagined that enemy planes would drop not only napalm but also 25 tons of oil-filled bombs per square mile, and that winds would race through the city at gale force.

It was too much for the crowded metropolis and for amateur fire fighters with their feeble streams of water from hand pumps, their straw mats soaked with water, their buckets of sand. Fragile houses flared up in minutes; families ran screaming into the streets or were buried in the fiery debris.

Police tried to lead people to firebreaks, to vacant lots or to blackened stretches where the fire had already consumed everything and burned out. A few hoses still worked, and the firemen turned those on the people to soak them before they struggled blindly through the flames. But utility poles had come down and snarls of electric power lines impeded the way. Blocked by a wall of flame, young Torao Okada covered his mother's back with a thin quilt. Then they both closed their eyes and ran until they had passed through the fire. Katsuko Yamamoto led her eight children to safety by tying them together; her eldest boy led the way and she brought up the rear with the youngest in her arms.

The fire became so hot and the smoke so thick that it burned the lungs, and people dropped in their tracks, writhing in agony. Before long, streets and alleyways were lined with rows of blackened corpses—people who had suffocated and burned as they sought to escape through tunnels of oxygen-sucking flames. In the gale-force winds, people who were well out of range of the flames caught fire from flying sparks. Clothing ignited. Mothers with babies strapped to their backs felt them catch fire.

In the midst of this holocaust, Masumi Taniguchi gave birth to her third child. She had entered a maternity hospital earlier in the evening, but it had to be evacuated when fire bombs bracketed the building. A doctor led Mrs. Taniguchi

The main buildings of the Imperial Palace lie in ruin after flames from an incendiary raid on downtown Tokyo leaped the moat and ignited them. The Emperor survived the raid in his bunker and emerged to thank the thousands of fire fighters who had tried to save the palace.

TAKING REVENGE ON CAPTURED ENEMY AIRMEN

The B-29 crews who bombed Japan did not go unscathed. In little more than a year of operations, approximately 300 Superforts were lost, and the crewmen who survived frequently found themselves in peril from vengeful Japanese. In the city of Fukuoka, Japanese Army officers routinely killed captured fliers. On one occasion, soldiers practiced deadly karate chops and sword cuts on eight airmen before decapitating them.

But some Army officers and policemen followed orders and did what they could to save downed Americans from being murdered by enraged Japanese civilians. The report of a policeman named Tsukamoto described one such effort. On May 5, 1945, Tsukamoto and a group of armed villagers raced to a small forest near the Tachiarai air base in Kyushu. A B-29 raiding the base had just burst into flames, and one of the plane's crewmen had parachuted into the trees.

Catching sight of the American, Tsukamoto called out in broken English, "Hold up, hold up." The young American understood and raised his hands, dropping his pistol to the ground. But then the villagers started screaming, "Kill him, kill him now!" Terrified, the American snatched his weapon from the ground, aimed it at his temple and pulled the trigger. He collapsed and died.

Tsukamoto stood over the body, fending off angry people who were trying to hack at it with swords and knives. An old woman with a carving knife struggled toward him shouting: "I had two sons drafted, and the Americans killed them both. I want my revenge!" But then she focused on the smooth face and tousled red hair of the American, who could not have been more than 20 years old. She dropped to her knees and shook his body, crying, "Why did you have to kill? Don't you have parents of your own?"

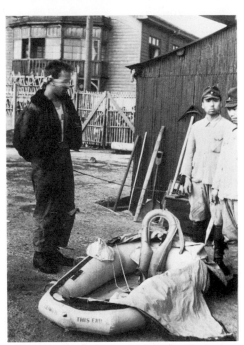

Blindfolded and hands bound behind him, a captured American flier stands beside his life jacket and inflated survival raft in Kobe.

After a raid, Japanese soldiers investigate the wreckage of an American B-29 strewn among the terraced fields of Hyogo prefecture, near the port of Kobe.

and others toward a shelter, but before they reached it her labor pains forced her to lie down on the bare, nearly freezing ground. There, with the help of three nurses, she gave birth to a boy. They wrapped him in her slip and stayed with her, watching the fires around them until dawn.

At another hospital, just as the sirens began blaring their first warning, a girl was born to Miyo Musha, the wife of an electrical-supply manufacturer and already the mother of 12 children. An hour later, the head nurse looked out and saw the sky bright with red patches, with black smoke trailing from the great flares and tidal waves of sparks rolling toward the hospital. Since the chief doctor was outside tending the injured, she ordered an evacuation.

Mrs. Musha and her baby were put on a stretcher and covered with quilts as protection from the flames. Then, along with other patients, they were carried from the hospital to a railway station half a mile away. Somehow, cocooned with her mother, the baby slept throughout the five hours it took them to get through the flames and burning debris to the crowded railway station. There, a few hours later, Mrs. Musha learned that her husband and their other 12 children had perished in the fire.

In northeast Tokyo, crowds flocked to the temple of Kannon, which they considered either fireproof—it had survived all of Tokyo's fires—or protected by its namesake goddess. But the great wooden structure caught fire, and its roof collapsed in a torrent of sparks, setting fire to the temple gardens and creating a vast funeral pyre. Not far away, in the red-light district of Yoshiwara, high metal gates were clanged shut to prevent the indentured women from escaping and the flames from invading. When the fire storm came, the houses ignited instantly; many of the women died that night with their clients. To the south, around Nihombashi, police directed fleeing people to the Meiji-za, a famous theater, to seek shelter. But the refugees choked for lack of air and then the stage curtain ignited, turning the huge structure into a crematorium.

The Sumida River promised relief from the fire storm, and thousands converged on its banks and flung themselves in its shallows. But in some areas both banks were aflame, and the heat raised the temperature of the water until many people were literally boiled or steamed to death. Others drowned when the tide came in. Still others were driven un-

der and drowned by the crowds swarming behind them, desperate to reach the water. Thousands more sought refuge on bridges over the river, but when the metal heated up they jumped in and were washed away.

The all clear sounded about 5 a.m. Those who had been lucky enough to escape the fire collapsed from exhaustion. Yoshiko Sugiura recalled later in a poem: "Escaping in the dawn from the air raid's sea of fire, I fell into a deep sleep on the street with my child." In some areas, the fires took four days to burn out.

On March 10 and for days afterward there were corpses everywhere: corpses in family groups, in neighborhood clusters, in stacks, piles and small mountains around the schools and hospitals. Charred babies clung to fallen mothers, sisters and grandmothers. Husbands and wives were fused together in a last embrace. Some corpses stood upright with legs braced and arms extended as if trying to run and escape the flames. An Army doctor picking his way along the Sumida River at daybreak found "countless bodies floating, clothed bodies, naked bodies, all as black as charcoal. It was unreal. These were dead people, but you couldn't tell whether they were men or women. You couldn't even tell if the objects floating by were arms or legs or pieces of burned wood."

While neighborhood associations struggled to find food and temporary shelter for the survivors, municipal authorities and volunteers helped Army units collect the dead. If the bodies could be identified, they were buried in marked graves; otherwise they were interred in mass plots of 100 bodies each. A Tokyo police chief, Yuichi Kori, stopped stock-still while clearing away corpses and stared at the burned figure of a man with a dead child strapped to his back. He silently asked their pardon, Kori later wrote, because the police had been unable to protect them.

On the 10th of March an exodus began for hundreds of thousands of survivors. They had no reason to stay. Their homes were ashes; roughly a quarter of a million houses had been destroyed, leaving 1.8 million people homeless. Gas, electricity, water and public transport had been shut down. Some refugees had lost everything and left empty-handed. Others salvaged bedding and utensils, found carts or wagons, and trudged out of town toward the homes of relatives in the country or anyone who would take them in. The railroads, which were repaired in miraculously short time, freighted out thousands more.

Later, the government tried to determine the number of dead in the 16 square miles of cooling ash. No one ever knew for sure, but conservative official estimates ran from 80,000 to 100,000 people. Earlier reports that more than 120,000 had died were suppressed. Robert Guillain, a French correspondent, saw Japanese documents reporting a total of 197,000 dead, or missing and presumed dead. A Home Ministry official explained why no accurate count was ever compiled: "We were instructed to report on actual conditions. Most of us were unable to do this because the conditions were horrifying beyond imagination."

Shortly after the raid, Emperor Hirohito made one of his rare excursions from the palace to see the city for himself. Despite objections from officers of the Imperial Household Agency, the Emperor insisted on being driven to the areas of worst destruction. In each sector he picked his way on foot through the rubble, to the astonishment of the citizens digging out. At the end of his two-hour tour, Hirohito somberly returned to his black sedan bearing the golden imperial chrysanthemum. He turned to a chamberlain and compared the devastation with the destruction caused by the great earthquake of 1923. "This seems infinitely more terrible," the Emperor said in a low voice. "Tokyo has become no more than scorched earth."

That was only the beginning of the horror, although no city thereafter suffered so many casualties in a single fire bombing. Four days later, on March 14, the B-29s unleashed their fury on Osaka, Japan's second largest city and a vital seaport. Ironically, one witness to the devastation there was an American Marine.

Private Martin Boyle had been captured on Guam at the beginning of the War, and when the B-29 raids commenced in November 1944, he was being held in Osaka Prisoner of War Camp No. 1, along with 450 fellow Marines and some British prisoners from Singapore. Boyle later wrote in his memoirs, *Yanks Don't Cry,* that he watched the bombing pattern develop "with mixed feelings of elation, respect, hero worship and some nervousness about the whole thing. It was something like living in a small town and having the

Downtown Osaka, devastated by incendiary bombs, was a vast sprawl of rubble in June of 1945. Even the streets had disappeared; "Everything," reported a survivor of the raids, "was a scorched wasteland."

World Champion Yankees come to play your home team—and clobber it."

The raids on Osaka increased steadily in size. Boyle watched four planes, then eight, then 16 and finally hundreds pummel the factories and military facilities of the huge Osaka-Kobe industrial complex. Wrote Boyle: "At the start, the bombers attacked only during the daylight hours; then, using the same deliberate pattern as in the day raids, the bombers began to attack at night, and the almost absolute silence of the Osaka nights emphasized the terrifying sound of the aerial bombs when they whistled over the prison camp sounding like a bunch of runaway freight cars. The air attacks never stopped—rain or shine, sleet or snow."

Boyle had his first narrow escape around Christmas 1944, the day after a big raid. He and his fellow prisoners, quartered on the Osaka waterfront where they labored as stevedores, were taken through the city to an Army storage dump where a bomb had scattered a large stack of empty oil drums. Their civilian foreman, whom they called Charlie-san, received work instructions from a Japanese officer and put the prisoners to work restacking the drums. "It was almost quitting time," Boyle recalled, "when the warning sirens started to wail, and Charlie marched us to a small building that fronted on a canal, where we were going to sweat out the raid."

It was a large-scale strike concentrated on a steel mill about a mile away. "The B-29s used heavy stuff on the larger targets, and the big bombs shook all the buildings around us when they bit into the mill. Toward the end of the attack a big bomb whistled right over the building we were in. We ducked when it hit the ground and exploded, and it felt like the whole building was coming down on top of us. I crawled over to the door and looked out and saw that the bomb had buried itself in a row of small wooden warehouses; two or three had caved in, and the nearest was on fire." Then the Marines learned that some Japanese children on the way home from school had taken cover in that warehouse when the siren sounded, and were trapped inside.

The prisoners rushed to the burning building. The door was blocked by timbers knocked down by the bomb. One Marine grabbed an iron bar to pry off the timbers while the others kicked away the burning rubble. They got the door open and all the children tumbled out unharmed.

By January 1945, attacks by U.S. carrier-based planes and submarines on Japanese shipping offshore had made Osaka a ghost harbor; it had been months since Boyle and the other prisoners had seen a really big cargo ship. But the B-29s continued to come, concentrating on basic industry: the manufacturing plants on the perimeter of the Osaka-Kobe harbor complex, and the steel mills, warehouses and storage dumps that supplied them. On March 14, the American planes dealt Osaka its worst punishment.

Bombing by radar through heavy cloud cover, 274 B-29s blanketed the port city with 1,733 tons of incendiaries. During the furious fire storm that followed, 134,744 houses were destroyed. Effective firebreaks and decentralized workers' housing helped to limit the casualties. After the raid, the Osaka fire department listed 4,000 people dead, twice that number injured and about 500 missing.

Four days later, on March 18, Nagoya was the target, and this time American Naval aircraft from a carrier joined 300 B-29s in the attack. The onslaught left three square miles in ashes and sent thousands of refugees fleeing into the countryside. Many others made shift in their damaged homes. Some patched together shacks in the rubble. And some simply survived as best they could in the open.

After the March raids, the bombing continued to increase in frequency and range. From April through June the B-29s hit targets approximately every other day, and by July they were attacking two days out of every three. The cities were targets for fire bombing; the war plants, military bases, refineries, aircraft factories and the transport system were targets for both incendiaries and high explosives.

The B-29s flew missions beyond Tokyo, reaching 120 miles north to Koriyama and more than 200 miles to Sendai, on the northeast coast. They started to attack more than one target a day: Shizuoka, 85 miles to the southwest of Tokyo, Koizumi, 20 miles to the north, and Tachikawa, 20 miles to the west of the capital, were all bombed on April 4. Later the count rose to four and five targets or even more in a single day.

The port of Osaka was heavily hit on a day in May 1945. "By early afternoon," prisoner Boyle recalled, "the skies over Osaka were black with B-29s, and it was evident early in the raid that they were taking dead aim on the last major target left in the sprawling city, the waterfront. The bombardiers' sighting marks had finally crossed on us.''

Herded at bayonet point into a wooden-roofed brick warehouse at the harbor's edge, Boyle and a dozen other prisoners were appalled to find that the sergeant guarding them had chained and padlocked the iron door from the outside. ''We almost panicked when some incendiary sticks thudded on the wooden roof and set it on fire,'' he wrote. ''The fire spread quickly and big pieces of burning wood started dropping on the floor. The flames were already eating at the wooden rafters and we knew the roof wasn't going to stay up very long.'' The men formed a human pyramid so that one of them, Sergeant Josh Mackery, could clamber up, break a window and drop 20 feet to the alley outside, where he found an iron bar and pried off the lock and chain. Choking and stumbling through the smoke to the open air, the prisoners ran between the flaming wooden warehouses to a covered pier that extended out over the water. They discovered Japanese civilian stevedores huddled there, but the sergeant-warden and all the soldiers had disappeared—after telling the civilians that the POWs had been returned to their camp.

It took only an hour for the incendiaries to level every wooden structure along the docks and drop flaming roofs into the masonry buildings. One of the civilians volunteered to march the prisoners back to camp. ''Away from the docks,'' Boyle wrote, ''there was nothing to hold back or slow down the rampaging flames. And it was sheer chaos. The smoke and dust were so thick that we couldn't see half a block in front of us. A lot of the flimsy buildings were already flattened and big angry flames were making quick work of the rest. We had to walk in the middle of the street to avoid the flaming debris.'' One of the toughest of the Marines cried when he found a small boy's school cap in the smoking rubble. ''We were silent the rest of the way back to camp. When we got there, all that remained of Osaka Prisoner of War Camp No. 1 was the cinder-block foundation.''

Displaced, the POWs joined the general exodus to the countryside, where they spent the rest of their captivity reclaiming barren hillsides for rice planting.

The number of bombers over Japan continued to grow. Four hundred hit seven different targets on May 10, and on May 14 and 17 another 500 took part in each of two massive raids that left one quarter of Nagoya in ashes. More than 500 bombers hit different parts of Tokyo on May 24 and 26; in the latter raid, 4,000 tons of incendiaries left the center of the city burning for 36 hours.

The Imperial Palace fell victim to the May 24th raid, even though that expanse of buildings, shrines and gardens be-

In the aftermath of the worst fire-bomb raid on Tokyo, on March 10, 1945, homeless survivors stream out of the city while an Army band, at rear, persists in celebrating Armed Forces Day—despite the death of an estimated 100,000 people in the raid.

hind the great, gray stone moat in the city's heart was supposedly off limits to the bombers. Bursts of wind-blown flame from errant incendiary sticks set fire to the separate pavilions of the Dowager Empress and the Crown Prince, as well as a dozen other buildings inside the palace grounds. Nearly 10,000 soldiers, government workers and fire fighters, supported by 40 fire engines, fought the fires for about four hours. The soldiers were ordered to grab paintings and other art objects and carry them to safety. They saved much of value, but the battle against the flames was futile and eventually 27 buildings, including the main palace itself, were destroyed. The Emperor and his family were safe, having taken refuge in the special bomb shelter built for them under the Imperial Library.

The next day the Emperor and Empress picked their way through the ashes to thank those who had fought so hard to save the palace buildings. Several generals proposed to resign in ritual acceptance of responsibility for the disaster, but they were dissuaded by the Emperor.

When news of the palace's destruction was made public, the people were badly shaken. But the Emperor seemed pleased to have shared in the misery of his people, however briefly. He lived out the rest of the War in his bomb shelter.

In every city, the repeated bombings had a cumulative, nerve-shattering effect. Despite orders to the contrary, many workers fled to the countryside, swelling the number of refugees to nearly eight million by July. Those who had the resolve to stay in the cities lived in fear and despondency. The Americans preyed on the people's fears, dropping leaflets that announced which cities were soon to be attacked. The authorities denounced the leaflets and threatened a three-month jail sentence to anyone who failed to turn them in.

Many people had vivid, terrifying bombing nightmares. On the morning of June 15 in Osaka, Rie Kuniyasu's grown daughter told her that she had dreamed that a B-29 was chasing her through the city and she could not run away. Mrs. Kuniyasu urged her to stay home from work that day, but her daughter had to go because she had been entrusted with the key to the munitions plant. The bombers came again, and the daughter did not return home at the usual hour that evening. She still had not come back by three in the morning, so her frantic parents went into the city to look for her. When they finally reached the factory, they learned that their daughter had been caught in the open and killed by a bomb before she could reach a shelter. Her nightmare had come true.

Superstition was rife. A Tokyo couple who had escaped unscathed from their demolished house attributed their luck to the sacrifice of their two pet goldfish, found dead in the ruins. They took the goldfish to the local temple, and the story spread. Soon every live goldfish in Tokyo had been bought up at exorbitant prices, and a brisk business was being done in tinted ceramic goldfish. Eating a rice ball with a scallion inside it also was said to guarantee safety from the bombs and, in the face of all evidence, some people believed that once their neighborhood had been hit it would not be bombed again.

Many wild rumors went the rounds, and one of the saddest involved the city of Yokohama. The great port south of the capital had never appeared as a target on American bombing leaflets, and as months passed without a raid on the city, the people came to believe that it was to be spared because the Allies intended to use its docks in their invasion. In the hope that the city was a haven, long lines of refugees from Tokyo crowded the bomb-scarred highway to Yokohama. Ironically, it was downtown Tokyo that the Americans had crossed off their target list for incendiary attacks; after six major raids, the capital by the end of May was judged unworthy of further attention.

On May 29 the B-29s finally hit Yokohama in a daylight raid that lasted an hour and leveled half the city. Miraculously, only 5,000 people died. Once again the refugees fled, leaving the streets choked with abandoned household goods and furniture.

The largest coordinated air attack on Japan—2,000 aircraft in all—came on the 10th of July. More than 500 B-29s bombed five cities: Wakayama and Sakai near Osaka, the refineries in Yokkaichi near Nagoya, Gifu in the mountains behind Nagoya, and Sendai far to the north of Tokyo. One thousand planes from aircraft carriers pounded airfields around Tokyo, 300 planes hit airfields in Kyushu and the rest struck Osaka and Nagoya.

In Osaka, Tomie Akazawa was quick and lucky. With her husband, daughter and many of their neighbors, she sought safety from the flames near a large, recently built water tank. "Incendiary bombs ignited buildings, houses, even the grass in vacant lots," Mrs. Akazawa wrote later. "The flames caused tremendous updrafts that lifted our protective quilts from our shoulders." The heat and the smoke soon drove Mr. Akazawa frantic; he "threw himself into the water tank, where there were already countless refugees, some of them clinging to bicycles and even to live chickens." Then her daughter's padded hood caught fire. "I lifted her into the water tank and dragged myself in after her," Mrs. Akazawa recalled. "My husband ran away. He later thanked me over and over for saving our child and said that in times of great stress, men are useless."

The next day, Osaka was raided yet again. Fumie Masaki's husband, an engraver of wood and ivory, rushed from his shop as a plane droned overhead; he was sprayed by a falling incendiary that wrapped his body in a sheet of blue flame. "Neighbors carried him to a medical-relief center in a nearby school," Mrs. Masaki said. "His hair was still sizzling and giving off a blue light. His skin peeled away in sheets, exposing his flesh. I could not even wipe his body." She tended him through the agony of the night until he died in the morning.

Mrs. Masaki's tragedy was soon compounded. Two days later her son, who had been evacuated to the countryside, was playing with friends in a schoolyard when they found an unexploded bomb and reported it to an air-raid warden. The warden came to the playground, picked up the bomb and tossed it to see whether it was still live. It went off, killing eight of the children outright and fatally wounding Mrs. Masaki's son. She was notified and rushed to the place to find the boy still alive. When he saw her, he asked: "Where's Dad? How is he?"

She lied: "He's at home today. He's not feeling well."

The boy said: "I wish I could see him. Mother, I made a doll for the new baby. I left it with my teacher. Please go and get it."

A few minutes later, the boy died. Mrs. Masaki wrote later: "My kindhearted, bright little son never knew that his father had been killed. His father never knew that his child would follow him so soon in death."

The bombing went on and on until it seemed there was no longer anything left to destroy. By July the Americans had dropped nearly 90,000 tons of bombs on Japan and had burned out 127 square miles of 26 cities. About 2.5 million buildings had gone up in flames. Overall industrial production had dropped to 40 per cent of the peak output of 1944; coal production had been cut in half; oil refining had been reduced to 15 per cent, aircraft-engine production to 25 per cent, ordnance and explosives production to 45 per cent, aluminum output to 9 per cent.

By the end of July, nearly 500,000 Japanese had been killed in the air attacks. Another 13 million people had been displaced from their homes. The casualty figures did not include the innumerable people who perished of malnutrition, tuberculosis or other diseases that were brought on by exposure or lack of food.

In the cities, life was a series of miserable makeshifts. In Tokyo, whose population had been reduced by about four million since 1940, no more than 2.5 million people remained. They subsisted in what had become a collection of small villages centered around wells, canals, clusters of masonry buildings, railway terminals and a few unscorched areas. Water and gas mains had been ruptured beyond repair; people drew water from ancient wells and boiled it over open fires. The Army released some of its hoarded rice stock, but the supply did not go very far, even when it was mixed with coarser grains and seeds. People scratched out little gardens wherever they could find bare earth, and they trapped sea gulls scavenging among the ruins. Hardly any carts or bicycles remained; occasionally, charcoal-burning trucks and cars moved about. But only a few main thoroughfares had been cleared of rubble; there were not enough people left to do the rest of the job.

The one thing that still worked with some regularity was the national railway system, and the one thing that the government was able to do for the homeless was to give them free rail tickets to wherever they cared to go. Dirty, ash-blackened refugees scattered through the countryside like flocks of starlings, adding to the rural overcrowding.

Wherever they subsisted, the people of Tokyo and of every bombed-out city now shared a sustaining passion that went beyond patriotism. "In the heart of the ordinary Japanese," journalist Masuo Kato recorded, "there was hatred and bitterness toward the American raiders who left an indiscriminate trail of the blackened corpses of babies and grandmothers among the wreckage of war."

DEsTRUCTION FROM THE SKY

Japanese searchlights pin a B-29 Superfortress in their cross beams as packets of incendiaries explode, raining flame on the city of Sakai on July 10, 1945.

A CITY CONSUMED BY WIND-WHIPPED FLAMES

In the early-morning darkness of March 10, 1945, more than 250 B-29s loosed some 2,000 tons of incendiary bombs over Tokyo. The raid was the first major test of a new tactic by General Curtis LeMay, head of the XXI Bomber Command. Earlier sorties against Japan—the 1942 Doolittle raid and the high-altitude precision bombing in 1944—had done little damage. LeMay now planned to cover Japan's industrial cities with fire from low-flying planes.

The Tokyo fire bombing set a grisly pattern for widespread fire raids against a number of cities that followed. Incendiaries fell in the most densely populated part of Tokyo, the Koto district, a workingman's quarter where 103,000 people per square mile lived packed together in houses of wood, bamboo and rice paper. A cold, freakish wind was blowing at 40 miles an hour, and journalist Masuo Kato recalled that it "whipped hundreds of small fires into great walls of flame, which began leaping streets, firebreaks and canals at dazzling speed." The hurricane of fire outdistanced, surrounded and incinerated countless Japanese who tried to flee. Many who were not burned to death died of asphyxiation. "The flames roared on," Kato reported, "gulping great drafts of oxygen, and thousands of human beings died in shelters, in the streets, in the canals and even in large open areas, like so many fish left gasping on the bottom of a lake that has been drained." To escape the leaping balls of flame, throngs of people jumped into the Sumida River and the narrow canals that crisscrossed the district.

The heat was so intense that the air currents it created bounced 90-foot-long B-29s thousands of feet upward, and the fire was so bright that tail gunners could see the glow from 150 miles away as their planes sped back to bases in the Marianas. In one night, 16 square miles of Tokyo had been leveled, and the fires raged for four more days.

Following this first success, the B-29s obliterated great areas of Nagoya, Osaka, Kobe and dozens of other industrial centers. In block after block of the stricken cities, all that remained were smoldering telephone poles—what a Tokyo woman called "grave markers in the wasteland."

Citizens of Tokyo inspect one of the 50 houses destroyed by the 1942 Doolittle raid. Only a handful of people were killed in this early air attack.

In Tokyo's busy Ginza section, people seek shelter in doorways and an uncovered trench as an unseen U.S. reconnaissance plane buzzes overhead.

A cluster of incendiaries detonates over Osaka in March of 1945, spreading the already glowing fires.

CANISTERS OF NAPALM, RIVERS OF BURNING OIL

In laying waste to Japan's major cities, the B-29s followed a deadly efficient attack pattern. The lead planes, called pathfinders, identified the target area and dropped their payloads to mark the spot. The bomb used to ignite the initial blaze was usually the M-47, a 70-pound canister that was fused to explode 100 feet above ground and scatter dozens of cylinders two feet long containing napalm, a jellied gasoline. The cylinders released flaming napalm on impact with the tinderbox houses, kin-dling a profusion of small fires that quickly united and spread.

The bombers that followed homed in on the flames below and loosed another type of incendiary, the M-69, which contained oil. These six-pound bombs were dropped in clusters that also exploded overhead with an incandescent brilliance. As the oil rained down, the first drops were ignited by the blazing napalm below and sheets of fire burst upward. Then the flames settled to earth and flowed in streams through the streets of the doomed Japanese cities. The bombers that were still farther back in line then fanned out to feed the edges of the growing conflagration.

Fountains of fire dance in the streets of Osaka on March 14 as incendiaries stream down through the night sky. This single raid consumed 134,744 houses.

A storm of fire rages through downtown Osaka during the March 14 raid, fueled by 1,733 tons of incendiaries dropped by 274 attacking B-29s. The flimsiness

of the buildings helped the fire to spread; in one area, racing flames have consumed the thin board walls of houses, briefly silhouetting their wooden frames.

Soldiers, police and air-raid wardens rush toward Kobe's disaster area on June 5, 1945.

Firemen battle to save a house in Kobe on June 15. But

A bucket brigade doggedly relays sea water from Kobe's beach toward the blazing city.

they could do little, since previous bomb damage had knocked out much of the municipal water system, lowering the city's water pressure by 70 per cent.

"THE BEST THING TO DO WAS RUN FOR YOUR LIFE"

The Japanese were helpless to combat the incendiary-bomb attacks. City fire departments were overwhelmed by the towering walls of fast-moving flame. Neighborhood volunteers dutifully battled the fires—and lost their lives in the process. Homemade air-raid shelters became deathtraps where thousands suffocated. A girl said simply, "The best thing to do was pack up and leave—run for your life."

Innumerable Japanese did run—but in vain. "On some broad streets, as far as one could see," journalist Masuo Kato reported after the Tokyo raid, "there were rows of bodies where men, women and children had tried to escape the flames by lying down in the center of the pavement. There were heaps of bodies in schoolyards, in parks, in vacant lots and huddled under railroad viaducts."

Soldiers and civilian rescue workers use grappling hooks to fish bodies from Tokyo's Sumida River, where thousands were drowned, suffocated or boiled to death trying to find refuge from the smoke and flames.

Piles of corpses, charred beyond recognition, lie in a Tokyo street after the March 10 fire raid. It took the survivors 25 days to collect and dispose of the remains of citizens killed during that single catastrophic attack.

6

One last battle—and another, and another
Bracing to face an Allied invasion
A diet of weeds and worms
"I will sacrifice even my children"
Seeking victory through suicide
A search for exits from the War
The Emperor's silent plea
A peace Cabinet harnessed to an old war horse
Dead end in Moscow, deaf ears in Washington

"If Japan wins on Leyte, we win the War!" So said Prime Minister Kuniaki Koiso in a radio address to the nation on November 8, 1944. Huge American forces had invaded Leyte, and the chiefs of staff of the Imperial Army and Navy had agreed to stake all of their resources on a battle to hold the central Philippine island. Koiso called the struggle for Leyte a *Tennozan,* referring to the epochal battle at Tennozan in 1582 in which a feudal leader had staked the entire course of his war for national supremacy on the outcome of a single engagement. The word denoted to everyone in Japan that a final, winner-take-all battle was under way.

As early as October 25, however, only five days after the first U.S. troops set foot on Leyte, one third of Japan's Combined Fleet had been destroyed in the Battle for Leyte Gulf; and that disaster had made the loss of Leyte a strategic certainty. This had not been explained to Koiso, and as late as December 20, he was still talking of a victory on Leyte. But on his way to an audience with the Emperor, the War Minister, General Hajime Sugiyama, whispered in his ear, "Prime Minister, I should tell you that the high command has decided to abandon its strategy for a decisive battle on Leyte in favor of an all-out decisive battle on Luzon."

Before Koiso could recover from the shock, he found himself facing the Emperor, who pointedly asked him if he was aware that the high command had decided to abandon Leyte for Luzon.

"I did not know about it until just before I came for this audience with Your Majesty," Koiso replied.

The Emperor leaned forward and said with suppressed anger, "Prime Minister, have you thought of a way to justify your statement that the Leyte battle was a *Tennozan?*"

Flushed with embarrassment and rage, Koiso bowed out of the room. He was in despair. How could he hope to run the government when the most elemental facts about the War were denied him? What other bad news was being withheld by the high command?

Worse was to come. The Japanese defeat on Luzon was followed by other failed *Tennozan*—Iwo Jima in March 1945 and Okinawa in June. More and more it became apparent that the ultimate *Tennozan* would be the defense of Japan itself.

At this point Koiso and other practical leaders realized that the War had been lost, and they began to put out peace

LOST BATTLES, LAST HOPES

feelers. Tragically, Japanese pride and Japanese tradition made it impossible for them to sue for peace in terms intelligible to the Westerners. Preparations for the battle of Japan went forward.

In planning for the last battle, the Army leaders honestly believed that the Americans had shot their bolt, that a single, devastating defeat might yet persuade them to abandon the War. In persisting in this view, they disregarded two facts: that U.S. submarines had sunk most of Japan's merchant fleet and had reduced vital imports of fuel, food and raw materials to a trickle, and that U.S. planes were bombing Japan's industrial cities to rubble.

On February 6 at Ichigaya, headquarters in Tokyo of the Imperial Japanese Army, the new policy of defending Japan was made official by the Army's chief of military operations. Lieut. General Shuichi Miyazaki gave the assembled department chiefs of the general staff a realistic briefing on the impending loss of the Philippines, but declared: "We shall turn the tide of the War by meeting the enemy on the homeland, for which we are now preparing 16 new divisions. By pouring 20 divisions into the battle within two weeks of the enemy's landing, we will annihilate him entirely and ensure a Japanese victory."

The next day Miyazaki conferred with the commanders of Japan's six military districts, dividing among them the 16 new conscript divisions to be trained and whatever troops could be brought home from Manchuria. It was hoped, he said, that three Japanese soldiers could be committed against every Allied soldier who landed in any district.

The commanders anticipated that the most likely invasion routes were across the Sea of Japan from the Chinese mainland or northward from Okinawa. They designated the southern island of Kyushu as the main defensive front, with all preparations to be completed by summer. No sacrifice, they agreed in unison, would be too great. Gyokusai—the smashing of precious jade to prevent it from falling into unworthy hands—would be the fate of all Japan if final victory could not be won.

The Army began to make public its plans for the defense of the home islands later in February. General Miyazaki told a civilian gathering: "The course of the War will at last force the enemy to meet us on our own soil. Since the retreat from Guadalcanal, the Army has had little opportunity to engage the enemy in land battles. But when we meet in Japan proper, our Army will demonstrate our invincible superiority."

A three-day meeting of senior Army officers at the end of February refined plans for the battle. Staff officers promised that 40 divisions would be available in time to meet the expected invasion and estimated that 1.5 million additional men could be recruited if age limits were extended. The main feature of the defense was to be a series of counterattacks aimed at the expected invasion beaches. Great waves of Japanese soldiers would push the enemy back into the sea in what would surely be one of the bloodiest battles in the history of mankind.

In early March, the Army leaders persuaded Prime Minister Koiso to close all secondary schools; the students were swiftly mobilized to grow food, produce munitions, help with air-raid defenses and train under Army veterans to repel the invaders. The next step was to form the People's Volunteer Army, in which all men and women from the ages of 13 to 60, except for the sick and the pregnant, were organized to take up weapons when the invasion came. Since the general staff was unwilling to distribute rifles and ammunition among the people until the last moment, the training would be conducted with wooden rifles, dummy munitions and bamboo spears.

With proper ceremony, the Army continued to organize new divisions of raw youths and aged veterans. The Emperor, wearing all his military decorations, presented each new regimental commander with his unit colors. At a mass assembly on May 23 he handed out 40 new regimental flags. Tokyo radio claimed that 20 million students had been mobilized for "active combat duties." Farmers were also organized into an agrarian militia.

Tens of thousands of veteran troops were brought home from Manchuria and Korea to strengthen the nation's defenses. The soldiers swarmed over the countryside digging trenches and building forts; in the process they destroyed gardens, rice fields and even private homes. They overloaded the trains and crowded the public places, and their officers sometimes behaved toward Japanese civilians as arrogantly as they had toward the Koreans and Chinese. Junior officers were assigned to factories to "instill discipline.'' Their lectures and parade-ground manner only alienated the exhausted workers, and their efforts to impose military efficiency on factory routine served only to disrupt rather than streamline production.

On the 6th of June the general staffs of the Army and Navy presented to the War Council the final, formal plan for the last battle, a document that was entitled ''The Basic Policy for the Future Conduct of the War.'' Japan, the plan contended, had two important advantages: its rugged island geography and its loyal, united people. Lieut. General Torashiro Kawabe, the Army's Vice Chief of Staff, said that when the enemy tried to invade Japan, ''he will be met at the point of landing by an overwhelming Japanese force that will continue its attack until he is defeated and turned back.'' The plan called for destroying one fourth of the American landing force while it was at sea and another quarter on the beach during the landing.

Though the Army leaders hoped that the killing and maiming of enormous numbers of Americans would bring about a negotiated peace at the shoreline, they actually anticipated a long fight to the finish, with scorched-earth tactics and guerrilla warfare carried on from the mountains and caves of the home islands. They pointed out that the Japanese would have short lines of supply and communication, whereas those of the Americans would be long and vulner-

able. The Japanese would outlast and exhaust the invaders.

According to the Army chiefs, 2.5 million soldiers were now available for frontline combat, backed by four million civil servants with military training. Some 28 million men and women would be called up in a national mobilization and armed with rifles, grenades, even bows and arrows, if need be. Finally, the chiefs asserted that Japan still had some air power with which to attack the invaders. The Army claimed 7,000 planes, the Navy nearly 6,000. (Only a quarter of these planes were in fact first-line combat aircraft; the rest were obsolete models and training planes suitable only for suicide missions, and 5,225 of them were designated for this purpose.)

The War Council formally agreed to the plan two days later. At this final, ritualistic meeting, the Prime Minister gave a blunt summary: ''Japan's situation at the present moment is indeed critical; she has reached the point where she must pull continued life out of the jaws of death. This cannot be accomplished by either wisdom or skill—we must simply surge forward to our final goal.''

The Army made it clear that death or disgrace were the only alternatives to victory. Army propagandists released scare stories alleging that Allied invaders were committing atrocities as they overran Axis countries in Europe. The high command sent the secret police on a witch hunt for the fainthearted. More than 400 prominent citizens, including diplomats and judges, were arrested on suspicion of talking or even thinking about peace. Vague threats were voiced against those who did not—or even could not—help the national effort. A military police chief in Osaka went so far as to say, ''Because of the nationwide food shortage and the imminent invasion of the home islands, it will be necessary to kill all the infirm old people, the very young and the sick. We cannnot allow Japan to perish because of them.''

Their senses told the ordinary people of Japan that death in one form or another awaited them in the not-so-distant future—by fire bombing, by privation, by illness, or in the immolation urged on them by their military leaders. As the Army's last-ditch preparations went forward, the people's daily misery increased. Tuberculosis was rampant and pneumonia swept away many—not only the old and very

General Kuniaki Koiso, whose fierce appearance earned him the nickname ''Tiger of Korea'' when he served there as Governor General, was declawed by the Army general staff when he replaced General Tojo as Prime Minister in 1944. The general staff delayed telling Koiso about operational plans and denied him access to secret data.

young, but also once-robust adults who had been left exposed to the elements by the bombing of their homes.

In letters, diaries, memoirs and postwar interviews, the people told of their anguish. Hunger was everywhere; it dominated life. By June, food had become so scarce and people so poor that even the black market had begun drying up. School children evacuated to the country collected weeds and ferns to be boiled for food; people lived on this rough harvest even though the weeds cut their mouths and tasted awful. If a meal included meat, it was likely to be from a dog or cat, though everyone pretended it was squirrel or rabbit. One young girl dutifully ate the shark meat her father regularly got from a relative living near the coast, and it saved her from the vitamin deficiencies that many suffered. But she thought as she ate: "When the ships were torpedoed or bombed, so many people must have been eaten by the sharks. This is as bad as eating human flesh! And it smells so horrible!"

Silkworms removed in the processing of cocoons were boiled and eaten. Insects from the fields were collected, roasted and eaten. These insects and the dried residue from soybean-oil presses were the only protein most people got. Even with these substitutes for the government rice rations, most of them of questionable value and many of them indigestible, few people were getting the 1,200-calorie daily intake decreed as sufficient to keep people working.

The families of Japanese diplomats had better diets than most, but one official's wife worried constantly about their ill effects. "The three of us were growing much weaker. I had lost my physical energy and suffered from a mental lethargy that made me very forgetful. When one starves slowly, it is not a spectacular thing." Many solicitous parents gave part of their small rations to their children, and some of these parents weakened and died.

Most of the Japanese people were so exhausted physically that they did not expect to see another spring or even to survive the next air raid. They were exhausted spiritually as well; the moral fabric of the nation was breaking down. Robbery, pickpocketing and theft were common. Adults stole school children's lunch boxes, and looted neighbors' bombed-out homes. In air-raid shelters and relocation terminals, people had their last belongings stolen. The slogans, the drills, the enforced parades and assemblies that had been part of their lives since the invasion of China in 1937 now affected only the young and the simple. Most people merely prayed for an end to their suffering.

And yet most of the people of Japan were fully prepared to fight the invaders when they appeared. Women, the young and farmers—those who were secure in their patriotism and still had a little physical stamina—intended to sell their lives dearly in hand-to-hand defense of their soil. Some of the women were especially fierce in their determination; others were calmly idealistic. Sachiko Ishikawa, one of the few survivors of a volunteer nursing unit on Okinawa, later explained why she and her classmates had been ready to die: "It was the kind of education that we received earlier that made our great sacrifices possible. When we left school, one of our teachers told us that we did not have to

A crew practices launching an intercontinental balloon at a test site to the west of Tokyo.

SECRET WEAPONS CARRIED ON THE WIND

While Japan's cities shook and burned under American bombs, the Japanese sought a measure of revenge with a secret weapon they had developed: intercontinental balloon bombs.

Many of the balloons were constructed by nimble-fingered schoolgirls who used needles, thread and paste made from the devil's-tongue plant, a potato-like root native to Japan, to fit together 600 separate sheets of an extra-strong tissue.

In November 1944, the first wave of the bomb-laden balloons was released into the jet stream, which bore them at high altitudes across the Pacific Ocean. But the ingenious aerial assault was a flop. Of some 9,000 balloons eventually launched, only a few hundred reached North America, and they caused almost no damage.

stay with the corps and the troops; we could go home to relative safety. We replied that if necessary we were prepared to die for our country. It would be all right as long as Japan won the War."

A young housewife, undiscouraged by the bombing and privation, said grimly, "I have never thought of quitting. I will sacrifice even my children and fight to the death." A schoolgirl admitted that she was discouraged, but added: "If the government says 'Fight!' and if the rest of the girls fight, I'll fight."

The civilians were trained for their last heroic effort by drillmasters, whom the Army supplied to volunteer associations, schools, factories, government offices and farm communities. Each morning before dawn the citizens would line up for the day's training. In most areas the civilian defenders first paid a group visit to the local Shinto shrine to dedicate themselves anew to the Emperor, to their country and to the hundreds of thousands of Japanese who, by dying in battle, had become sacred spirits watching over the fate of Japan.

Strenuous calisthenics followed the spiritual exercises, then the groups lined up in front of life-sized targets made of straw bundles bound to sturdy uprights. Long bamboo poles, their ends honed to a point and hardened in fire, were distributed. To the commands of the drillmaster, men and women, old and young lunged, parried and thrust for an hour or so, shouting invective at the imaginary foe.

A high-school girl named Yukiko Kasai, who lived in Shimane prefecture on the coast of the Sea of Japan, was given a carpenter's awl by her teacher and told that when the Americans came, "we must be ready to settle the War by drawing on our Japanese spirit and killing them. Even killing just one American soldier will do. You must use the awl for self-defense. You must aim at the enemy's abdomen. Understand? The abdomen. If you don't kill at least one enemy soldier, you don't deserve to die."

A group of Tokyo girls who had been evacuated to the safety of the countryside became adept with the long, hook-bladed *naginata* spear, a weapon of medieval origin. In ex-

ercises the girls, swinging the light staffs with practiced ease, would rap the leg of local village boys armed with blunt *kendo* staffs, tumbling them to the ground before the boys could strike a blow. With the blade attached, the scythelike weapon was supposed to disable an enemy soldier by cutting off his leg.

New recruits in the Army dug foxholes, all the while carrying heavy weights on their backs. The weight-carrying was practice for an assignment the men had volunteered to undertake. After the American invasion, they would conceal themselves with 35-pound bombs strapped to their backs. When an enemy tank appeared, a single soldier was to race forward from his hiding place and hurl himself and the bomb under the tank. It would be a heroic death.

Small groups of conscripted students and older men built pillboxes and strung barbed wire along the shores; when the time came, they were supposed to fight the invaders as guerrillas. But they were woefully unprepared. Thirteen-year-old Susumu Nagara reported that his 20-man squad, assigned to dig ammunition caches in the mountains overlooking the Inland Sea, had only a single rifle: The weapon was rotated daily so that each man took a turn carrying it. Few of the men had ever fired a shot.

The many shortcomings in training and equipment apparently did not disturb the Army leaders. In June, General Korechika Anami, the Minister of War, proclaimed that "the sure foundation for victory" had been laid. At about the same time, home-front radio broadcasts assured the people that secret weapons had been readied to repel the Americans offshore.

The secret weapons were suicide planes and manned torpedoes, which already had been launched with frightening effect against the U.S. Navy. In case the gods failed to bring a *Kamikaze*—a Divine Wind—to destroy the invaders, the Army and Navy were raising their own storm of human Kamikazes to rain destruction on the enemy ships and landing craft with hundreds of explosives-packed fighter planes, and manned rocket-bombs and torpedoes. Training planes and ancient biplanes were being trucked into the mountains overlooking all likely invasion routes. The aircraft would be fueled by alcohol crudely refined from pine stumps. The planes would be laden with bombs and guided by volunteers with little flying experience; they would slide down long, steep ramps, hurtle into the air and crash on American ships and landing craft. Students and enlisted volunteers were being trained for this operation on Mount Hiei, above the city of Kyoto.

The term Kamikaze was applied to all suicide volunteers, whether flying planes, carrying bombs or manning torpedoes, but the ones who most stirred the imagination of the Japanese and inspired their spirit of sacrifice were the pilots. The suicide fliers wrapped white scarves about their necks and flew off in every sort of aircraft, usually with each plane carrying a single, 550-pound bomb. Many of them were university students in their early 20s who had been drafted when their deferments were revoked. They tended to be students of the humanities; engineering and science students were permitted to remain in school. Most were thoughtful young men who had calmly decided to sacrifice their lives for their country.

When the director of training at a torpedo-boat base offered his men a chance to volunteer for suicide missions, he

Air-raid survivors, living in an improvised shelter after fire bombs had completely destroyed their Tokyo neighborhood, go about their morning chores in the spring of 1945.

Schoolboys struggle to carry a pine stump that they have just pried out of the ground to be rendered for crude aircraft fuel. The work of uprooting stumps was the toughest of all the "volunteer" labor imposed on civilians.

carefully explained, "You must make this choice in all freedom, and I promise that no influence or pressure will be exerted on those men whose conscience prevents them from subscribing to the new form of attack. You will come one by one into my office to let me know your decision, and I give you my word that I shall put no questions to you nor ask for any sort of explanation." Half of the class, about 150 men, volunteered. The other half declined, without suffering penalty or censure.

As the situation grew worse, however, senior officers became more pointed in their requests for volunteers. The commanding officer of an airfield in Kyushu summoned two dozen pilots and told them he had been ordered to form a Kamikaze unit. He said: "I am obliged to ask you to volunteer for this mission. But you are free to choose." For most of them, this was the first time in their military service that they had been asked to do anything; before, they had always been ordered. Impressed by the appeal, they volunteered to the last man.

The spirit of the Kamikaze burned bright in the farewell poetry, letters and diaries that the pilots left behind. Through all their recorded thoughts ran a single theme: Duty, far more than hatred of the American enemy or desperate hope of salvaging a seemingly lost cause, sustained the Kamikazes in their hour of trial. One Naval officer volunteered to die even though he fully expected that Japan would be defeated. He said: "A man must do what he can for his country."

Many Kamikaze pilots thought of their sacrifice as repayment of a cultural debt. In a letter to his father just before he took off, Teruo Yamaguchi wrote: "The Japanese way of life is indeed beautiful. That way of life is the product of all the best things that our ancestors have handed down to us. It is

an honor to be able to give my life in defense of these beautiful and lofty things." Susumu Kaijitsu wrote: "Words cannot express my gratitude to the loving parents who reared and tended me to manhood that I might in some small manner reciprocate the grace that His Imperial Majesty has bestowed on us."

Inspired by such thoughts, the pilots lived out their last days in spartan purity. They indulged in no carousing with liquor or drugs, and the only women they saw were delegations of schoolgirls who came bearing flowers or cherry blossoms to bid them a formal farewell. For the most part, according to their last letters to loved ones, the young pilots slept deeply the night before their final flight, awakening refreshed and eager to go.

The Kamikaze spirit was held up as an example for every civilian to follow in the coming battle of annihilation. Susumu Nagara, the teenager at work digging ammunition caches above the Inland Sea, was prepared to die—and soon. He wrote years later that he repeatedly wondered, "How will it be to grapple with an enemy soldier and die?" And he wondered what would happen after he was killed. "Will I live with my parents? What will happen to my little brothers and sisters? How will they find the way to the Buddhist paradise where my parents and I will go when we die in battle?"

Individually and in their millions the Japanese prepared themselves mentally to take up their weapons and to try to kill at least one enemy soldier before dying. Some people recognized the pathetic contrast between their spear drills and the silvery B-29s soaring overhead, but that recognition made them no less fervent in their practice sessions. They would fight on their shores and in their streets and hills until an exhausted and blood-drained enemy halt-

Kamikaze pilots pass the time quietly at board games and music while they await their suicide assignments in 1945. A shortage of operational planes caused some volunteers to wait months before making their final flight.

ed the fighting and left their islands and their way of life intact. "Victory in the last five minutes" became the slogan of those who still had hope. For those who had no hope, *gyokusai* offered brittle comfort—their world would come crashing down with them.

The Emperor, in whose name millions of Japanese were preparing to die, was in fact chief among those in Japan who wanted to stop the fighting. He had acquiesced reluctantly in the launching of the War and he had seized on the idea of seeking peace as early as February 1942, when it was broached to him by his closest adviser, Marquis Koichi Kido, the Lord Keeper of the Privy Seal. Since that moment Hirohito had on many occasions suggested that his ministers end the War.

But a seemingly insurmountable obstacle to peace was the Allies' demand for the unconditional surrender of Japan, made public in December 1943 in the Cairo Declaration. Over the years, none of the avowed or secret proponents of peace had been able to devise a way to propose to the Allies a settlement that preserved Japan's "national essence," which meant primarily the ancient and sacred institution of the Emperor. The national essence included the "Japanese way of life," the inviolability of the home islands and, for the militarists, the honor of the Army, which they regarded as an extension of the Emperor's integrity.

From 1942 on, small groups of statesmen, bureaucrats and even military men pondered the problem of reconciling Japan's war aims with its dwindling capacities, and wrestled with the mechanics of opening a way to a negotiated peace. In one way or another, most of them were in touch with Marquis Kido and, through him, with the Emperor.

Not long after Kido's initial conversation with the Emperor on the subject, Foreign Ministry official Shigeru Yoshida, a quiet advocate of peace, suggested to Kido that Prince Fumimaro Konoe, a former Prime Minister well known in the West, be sent to Switzerland to look for opportunities to negotiate a peace. Konoe, supported by Marquis Kido and two former Prime Ministers who had tried to keep Japan out of war, Admirals Mitsumasa Yonai and Keisuke Okada, considered this and other ways of seeking peace. But they were constantly thwarted by the Army and by their own resolve to preserve the Emperor's status at all costs.

Late in 1943, at Yonai's request, Rear Admiral Sokichi Takagi, a brilliant planning officer on the Navy general staff, secretly undertook a long-term assessment of Japan's objectives, achievements and prospects. Given access to secret files of the Navy and the several war-production ministries, Takagi examined air, Naval and merchant-marine losses, surveyed the nation's dwindling stocks and sources of raw materials, and estimated the capabilities of the enemy. The study, completed early in 1944, pointed to a single conclusion: Japan was headed for certain defeat; only a negotiated peace could save it from destruction.

But Takagi dared not bring the report to the attention of his superior, Navy Minister Shigetaro Shimada, who was so subservient to General Hideki Tojo that his fellow admirals scornfully spoke of him behind his back as "Tojo's aide-de-camp." Instead, Takagi privately briefed Admiral Yonai and a few friends, including his counterpart in the Army, Colonel Sei Matsutani.

As head of the Army's top-secret long-range planning staff, Matsutani ordered his most trusted aides to prepare an independent survey. The result was a paper that he candidly titled "Measures for the Termination of the Greater East Asian War." The paper projected the conditions likely to face Japan from 1944 on, with recommendations appropriate to several sets of circumstances. The preferred plan focused on the moment of Germany's expected collapse and strongly urged that Japan make a major effort to end the War at that point; thereafter the Allies could only grow more powerful and their terms harsher. The final plan provided for a last-ditch situation in which Japan would face a stark choice between annihilation and surrender; when that happened, Matsutani's realistic analysts argued, Japan must abandon all its objectives and achievements save one, the preservation of the Imperial House and the traditions on which it rested.

Matsutani circulated the secret report among top Army and Navy officers. He felt so strongly about his findings that he rashly took the report to Prime Minister Tojo and earnestly explained to him that Japan must seek peace before merciless surrender terms were imposed on it.

Tojo's reaction was short and fierce: He denounced Matsutani's study as enemy propaganda and ordered the upstart staff officer transferred to a frontline command in China, where he would have a good chance of dying in expiation of his cowardly, treasonous thoughts.

Eventually, Colonel Matsutani's friends managed to get him recalled from his frontline assignment, but the experience sobered the small group of staff officers and mid-rank Ministry officials who shared the secret knowledge of the downhill slide of Japan's resources and capabilities. Their seniors used the data as ammunition to engineer General Tojo's resignation as Prime Minister and to compile private reports for Marquis Kido. But the War continued to be prosecuted on the basis of the formal assessments prepared by the Army and Navy general staffs, and these staffs and their reports were imbued with General Tojo's never-say-die attitude.

With Tojo and Shimada out and the boldly pessimistic Admiral Yonai in as Navy Minister and Deputy Prime Minister, Takagi in September 1944 prepared for his new chief and protector an updated version of Colonel Matsutani's assessments and recommendations. At Yonai's request, the report also included Takagi's own thoughts on how to get the Army's cooperation in ending the War, an estimate of public reaction to surrender and—most dangerous of all—a strategy for reaching the Emperor and enlisting his personal efforts to achieve peace. But Takagi's draft peace strategies ran into the rock on which all such ideas foundered, the Allied demand for an unconditional surrender. It seemed certain that unconditional surrender would mean the end of the Emperor, and not even the most ardent peace advocate would consider that sacrifice.

In January 1945, the Emperor himself took a hand. Balked by constitutional restrictions and military objections from convening a conference of former Prime Ministers and members of his Privy Council—as he would have liked to do—he summoned the men individually during the month of February to discuss the progress of the War and the possibilities for peace. From former Prime Minister Tojo, now elevated to the rank of elder statesman, the Emperor got a lecture on the need for national unity and determination, and the opinion that the Americans could not keep up the intensity of their attack. Tojo pressed for an imperial command to the people to devote themselves wholly to the war effort, declaring, "With determination we can win!"

Quite the opposite advice came from Prince Konoe. "Japan," he said, "has already lost the War." Konoe's great fear now was that the hatred of America engendered by Japan's losses and the privations of the home front would lead the Japanese people and even the Army into a pro-Communist revolution. "From the standpoint of maintaining Japan's imperial system, that which we have to fear the most is not defeat itself, but rather the threat inherent in the possibility that a Communist revolution may accompany defeat," he concluded. "I am firmly convinced that we should seek to end the War as speedily as possible."

Between Tojo's "we can win" and Konoe's "we have lost," no consensus was possible, and the rest of the elder statesmen in their individual audiences failed to speak up about their misgivings. Thwarted again, the sovereign patiently commissioned yet another study, charging Admiral Kiyoshi Hasegawa to examine the state of the Navy's morale and its material prospects for stemming the American offensive. Hasegawa's private report echoed those of Admiral Takagi and Colonel Matsutani: Far from being able to win, Japan could not even defend itself.

But the war leaders and the military bureaucracy were driving Japan inexorably toward destruction even as Hasegawa, Konoe, Marquis Kido and other imperial confidants were seeking avenues of escape.

Prime Minister Koiso had become a helpless bystander in the Army-dominated leadership, and the few seeds of peace scattered abroad by his foreign minister had fallen on stony soil. After Iwo Jima fell and the Americans landed on Okinawa, Koiso was forced to resign. On April 5, four days after the Okinawa invasion, Moscow announced that it would allow its neutrality pact with Japan to expire in a year—a clear warning of a new calamity, war with the Soviet Union.

Early on that same evening, the elder statesmen were formally convened to choose a new Prime Minister. They found themselves dominated by General Tojo, still speaking as forcefully and dogmatically as he had when he was Prime Minister. The choice, he said again, was between unconditional surrender and all-out fighting to the bitter end. Tojo, representing most of the generals, wanted to continue the War; Marquis Kido, some of the senior admirals and most of the former Prime Ministers wanted peace. Yet in the muddle of voices that followed, the only consensus achieved was that the next Prime Minister and Cabinet must have the confidence of the people.

Intimidated by Tojo's implied threat that the Army might "go its own way," the statesmen again ducked responsibility for choosing peace or war and selected a compromise candidate for Prime Minister, Admiral Kantaro Suzuki, who was uncommitted either to pressing the War or to seeking peace. A retired hero of the Russo-Japanese War, Suzuki belonged to no faction, and he enjoyed the respect of the other leaders. But he was almost 80 years old and he had no desire to be Prime Minister. He remained reluctant even when Kido implored him to take the post "to save the nation."

Later that evening, Emperor Hirohito waited in his library for the Prime Minister-elect to appear. The Emperor was exhausted and near despair. Insomnia wracked his nights; his days were spent poring over reports from his ministers, summaries of cables from his embassies, transcripts of American broadcasts and, lately, frank assessments of the War, which Marquis Kido previously had kept from him on the principle that the monarch should remain above politics. Worst of all was the suffering of his people, which he had seen during tours of bomb-ravaged Tokyo. Hirohito had lost 15 pounds, and his hair and mustache were tinged with gray.

Shortly before 10 o'clock, the Emperor composed himself as the murmur of voices in the antechamber signaled

A MOUNTAIN FORTRESS FOR THE ELITE

In November of 1944, Japanese engineers and 2,500 Korean laborers began blasting a pit in the side of Mount Minakami near Matsushiro, 110 miles northwest of Tokyo. They thought they were building an underground warehouse for the Army. In fact the installation, in the form of a chambered tunnel six miles long, was to serve as the nation's command post in case of an Allied invasion.

One section of the redoubt, lined with beautiful cypress wood, was built to serve as the emergency home of the Imperial Family; adjoining caverns were intended to house the Imperial General Headquarters and 10,000 government employees.

By July 1945, construction was almost complete. The Army started to furnish the headquarters area, even installing a bathtub for the Emperor. But there the work stopped, for Hirohito refused to say whether he would leave Tokyo for the redoubt. Lord Privy Seal Koichi Kido, the Emperor's adviser, was more explicit; he never dreamed, Kido later said, of fleeing "to commit suicide in a cave" while the people fought and died to repel the invaders.

Instead, at Hirohito's behest, the Army reinforced the bomb shelter on the palace grounds in Tokyo. The cavernous complex at Matsushiro remained empty.

Entrance buildings of the uncompleted Imperial General Headquarters (top) lead into hollowed-out Mount Minakami. At bottom, cylindrical wall supports and power cables line one of the central corridors of the retreat.

that the new Prime Minister was ready to be presented. The door opened and the familiar figure of Admiral Suzuki bowed low before him.

With a rare smile and a slight gesture of his hand, the Emperor cut short the flowery greetings that poured from the old admiral's lips. Suzuki, bulky and stooped in his formal morning coat, his eyes hidden under bushy eyebrows and his mouth under a tea-strainer mustache, was a man closer to Hirohito than the Emperor's own father: For 10 years Suzuki had been the household chamberlain and now he was president of the Privy Council, the man Hirohito called "Dear Uncle" on all but the most formal occasions. The Emperor could have no more loyal or devoted a Prime Minister, nor one more revered by the people. The nation needed all those qualities, for the Emperor of Japan was determined that, by all means and at all costs, the War must be brought to a speedy end before even greater suffering and disaster befell the country.

Admiral Suzuki bowed even lower than before. Almost pleading, he recited the reasons he felt inadequate to the heavy task urged upon him by the Privy Council and the elder statesmen. He was too old; he had never been comfortable with politics; the contemplative philosophy of the Chinese sage Lao-tse was more to his liking than the hurly-burly of administration and practical diplomacy. "And, Your Majesty," he concluded, "I am so deaf that sometimes I cannot hear even when Your Majesty speaks to me."

The Emperor's reply was gentle but firm: "Your unfamiliarity with politics is of no concern, nor does it matter that you are hard of hearing. Therefore, accept this command."

No word of peace or war passed between the two men. Tradition dictated that the Emperor could not simply say, "Uncle, find a way to defy the generals and make peace," though he later admitted that was his thought. He felt certain that Suzuki would understand and take the unspoken charge to his heart. Then the audience was over.

If the new Prime Minister had divined Hirohito's desire for peace, he kept the thought buried so deep that it escaped the notice of his choice for Foreign Minister, 63-year-old Shigenori Togo. Togo had been Foreign Minister at the time of Pearl Harbor, and had left the Cabinet soon after in a show of opposition to Tojo's policies. He had been the chief consultant of the secret peace party ever since; and now,

summoned from his retirement home, he expected that he would have the full weight of the Cabinet behind him in openly seeking peace.

At a late-night meeting with the Prime Minister, Togo asked discreetly what views Admiral Suzuki had on the course of the War. "I think that we can carry on the War for another two or three years," was the bland reply. In stunned disbelief, Togo argued the facts of Japan's material impoverishment against Suzuki's stubborn belief in the power of the Japanese spirit. Suzuki shook off his arguments like a bulldog shedding water, and at last Togo shrugged his shoulders and told the Prime Minister that their views on the prospects of the War were so divergent that they could not possibly cooperate. He declined the appointment as Foreign Minister.

Suzuki protested, and for another half hour the two men

Admiral Kantaro Suzuki, chosen Prime Minister by the Emperor in April 1945 in the hope that he could negotiate peace, instead urged the nation to fight to the end. But his appeals, he claimed after the War, were an exercise in haragei, or belly talk: saying one thing while meaning another.

wearily pursued the argument. Suzuki tired first, and they parted with a promise to renew the discussion the following evening.

The next day, April 6, Togo was subjected to a series of entreaties from the elder statesmen and the Emperor's councilors, begging him to take the job, assuring him that Suzuki would see the light if he had not already done so, arguing that it was up to him to bring the old man around. Bending the Emperor's confidence as far as he dared, Marquis Kido's private secretary telephoned Togo to whisper: "It seems to me that the Emperor is considering ending the War."

Finally, Suzuki sat down again with Togo and said elliptically, "So far as the prospect of the War is concerned, your opinion is satisfactory to me."

This vague reassurance persuaded Togo that he would have a free hand in the conduct of diplomacy. He accepted the job and immediately put in train negotiations to prevent an attack by the Soviet Union and to determine whether Moscow would mediate a peace between Japan and the Western Allies. But Togo remained skeptical about his Prime Minister's commitment to peace.

And no wonder. Prime Minister Suzuki's public pronouncements on the War made him sound to Japan and the world as belligerent as any militarist. In his first public broadcast he declared: "The hour is here, my countrymen. Every individual man and woman must steel himself for what is to come. It is my personal wish that we all throw ourselves into the fields of combat, surging forward even over my own dead body, for I will sacrifice myself to the Empire's cause." Later he told the Diet: "The people of Japan are the loyal and obedient servants of the Imperial House. Should the imperial system be abolished, they would lose all reason for existence. 'Unconditional surrender,' therefore, means death to the 100 million: It leaves us no choice but to go on fighting to the last man."

While Suzuki postured and the Army staff made ever more frenzied plans for the final battle, the diplomats of the Foreign Ministry plodded doggedly after the mirage of Soviet mediation. They were repeatedly rebuffed by Foreign Minister Vyacheslav M. Molotov. Former Prime Minister Koki Hirota, who had also served as ambassador in Moscow, was directed to approach the young Soviet Ambassador to Japan, Jacob A. Malik, in a new effort to extend the Soviet-Japanese neutrality pact and explore the possibilities for peace.

Hirota tracked down Malik at a hot-spring resort in Hakone on June 3 and, over dinner and liqueurs, the two diplomats had an amiable but inconclusive chat about putting their countries' relations on a friendlier footing. Hirota wrote a desperately optimistic account of the talk for his chief, but when he tried to meet Malik again in Tokyo the Soviet Ambassador—on orders from Molotov—suddenly found himself too ill to reply.

The Emperor himself directed that Hirota persist, but Malik remained unavailable until June 24. This time Hirota was empowered to offer the Soviets the possibility of exchanging Japan's hard-won mineral resources in Southeast Asia for a new alliance.

Malik remained indifferent, and on June 29 Hirota returned yet again, this time with a virtual carte blanche and a formal proposal for a new nonaggression pact. Malik told Hirota that the Japanese proposal would be sent to Moscow by the usual trans-Siberian courier. But in Moscow, Molotov pretended not to know what Japanese Ambassador Naotake Sato was talking about when he twice tried to raise the subject of the Hirota-Malik conversations.

Although he was afraid to tell the Emperor what was going on, Foreign Minister Togo drew the correct conclusion: The Soviet Union was stalling. The avenue to peace through Moscow was a dead end.

In fact, not only Molotov but senior officials in Washington knew all about the Japanese overtures, for Malik was reporting promptly to Moscow by cable. The Americans, having long since cracked the Japanese diplomatic code, were meanwhile reading Togo's frantic messages to his Moscow embassy and Ambassador Sato's blunt replies urging surrender at any cost. The Emperor himself would again take a hand, with a personal message to be carried to Moscow by Prince Konoe.

But on July 17 the Allies would meet at the German town of Potsdam, where they would rivet into place their final plans to crush Japan and their terms for that nation's surrender. During their two-week conference, the Americans and the Russians would ignore Japanese signals that discreetly but perceptibly pleaded for an end to the killing and the destruction. The peacemakers' time was fast running out.

DAYS OF DESPERATION

A homeless family trudges out of Yokohama, a haven for refugees until U.S. bombers ravaged it on May 29, 1945. Raids that year displaced 10 million Japanese.

JAPAN'S FATE: FIRE, ASHES AND TEARS

Kneeling on a bleak hillside far from the ruins of her Tokyo home, 15-year-old Mimeko Kani plucked the last fragment of charred bone from the still-warm ashes of the funeral pyre. Her father had died during the night, victim of a too-long winter and a too-long war.

All morning Mimeko had begged and scrabbled among the farmhouses of the strange village for bits of charcoal and scraps of wood. All afternoon she had toiled to keep the fire hot enough to consume her father's emaciated remains in a final ritual purification. That task should have fallen to the eldest son, but there was no eldest son; Mimeko and her invalid mother were the only surviving members of the family. Laying the iron chopsticks aside, she bowed low, allowing her tears to mingle with the ashes.

Fire, ashes and tears were what the War had brought Japan by the early summer of 1945. Now only the gods stood between the people and national immolation.

The burned-out heart of Tokyo lay surrounded by the rusting wreckage of factories and shattered antiaircraft guns. In scores of bombed-out cities, gaunt, dirty survivors labored to repair a shattered war machine that had run out of fuel. Millions of fragmented families, like young Mimeko Kani's, were on the move, fleeing from the cities and the American bombers.

Every man and woman over the age of 13 now belonged to the People's Volunteer Army and was subject to the same harsh rules that governed soldiers. All were under orders to fight to the death, to abandon the wounded and to commit suicide rather than be captured.

On the beaches of Kyushu, the Army's preparations to meet an Allied invasion went fitfully forward. In the mountains surrounding the still-intact city of Hiroshima, Army engineers dynamited enormous holes for new fortifications. Inspecting the earth-and-wire beach defenses, journalist Masuo Kato found most of them "primitive and toylike, handmade and crude"—the work of farmers conscripted from their fields. "Japan was fighting only from habit," he said, "and because she did not know how to quit."

Their eyes damaged by the heat and smoke of incendiary fires, civilians receive first-aid treatment in the lobby of a movie theater in Yokohama.

Tokyo citizens bow at a makeshift shrine after a March fire bombing razed the Honganji temple and killed thousands of people in the surrounding area.

A SCROUNGING, MAKESHIFT EXISTENCE

Evacuated from a fire-bombed section of
Tokyo, families set up housekeeping in
a converted Army barracks in a nearby suburb.

Carrying babies bound to their backs, Tokyo
mothers rake scorched rice from the ashes of a
burned-out warehouse while others in the
background wait their turn. The 1944-1945 rice
crop was Japan's poorest in more than a
decade, and by June of 1945, rice had all
but disappeared from the civilian diet.

A salvage party of workmen at the Japan Oil Company's shattered
Amagasaki factory drags away the crumpled roof of a demolished oil tank.

ENDLESS VISTAS OF DESTRUCTION

An emaciated survivor of the fire-bomb raids on Yokohama attempts to build a shelter from charred sticks and other remnants of his home.

Two Japanese girls in the industrial city of Yawata gaze out over acres of ruins—workers' homes burned to the ground by B-29 incendiary bombs.

BIBLIOGRAPHY

Agawa, Hiroyuki, *The Reluctant Admiral: Yamamoto and the Imperial Navy.* Transl. by John Bester. Kodansha International, 1979.

Aikawa, Takaaki, *Unwilling Patriot.* Tokyo: The Jordan Press, 1960.

Anderton, David A., *B-29: Superfortress at War.* Charles Scribner's Sons, 1978.

Argall, Phyllis, "Life's Reports: Tokyo in Wartime." *Life,* September 21, 1942.

Baerwald, Hans H., *Japan's Parliament: An Introduction.* Cambridge University Press, 1974.

Barker, A. J., *Suicide Weapon.* Ballantine Books, 1971.

Beasley, W. G., ed., *Modern Japan: Aspects of History, Literature and Society.* University of California Press, 1975.

Benedict, Ruth, *The Chrysanthemum and the Sword.* Houghton Mifflin, 1946.

Bisson, T. A., *Japan's War Economy.* The Institute of Pacific Relations, 1945.

Borton, Hugh, *Japan's Modern Century: From Perry to 1970.* Ronald Press, 1970.

Boyle, Martin, *Yanks Don't Cry.* Pocket Books, 1963.

Brooks, Lester, *Behind Japan's Surrender.* McGraw-Hill, 1968.

Brown, Delmer M., *Nationalism in Japan.* Russell & Russell, 1955.

Buko, Shimizu, *A Record of Chichibu during the War.* Tokyo: Kikuragesha, no date.

Butow, Robert J. C.:
Japan's Decision to Surrender. Stanford University Press, 1954.
Tojo and the Coming of the War. Princeton University Press, 1961.

Carter, Kit C., and Robert Mueller, compilers, *The Army Air Forces in World War II: Combat Chronology, 1941-1945.* Albert F. Simpson Historical Research Center, Air University and Office of Air Force History Headquarters, USAF, 1973.

Cary, Otis, *Mr. Stimson's "Pet City"—The Sparing of Kyoto, 1945* (Moonlight Series, No. 3). Kyoto: Amherst House, Doshisha University, 1975.

"The Citizen-Subject . . . Tightens His Belt and Wipes Off His Smile." *Fortune,* April 1944.

Cohen, Jerome B., *Japan's Economy in War and Reconstruction.* The Institute of Pacific Relations, 1949.

Coox, Alvin, *Japan: The Final Agony.* Ballantine Books, 1970.

Craig, William, *The Fall of Japan.* Dell, 1967.

Craven, Wesley Frank, and James Lea Cate, eds., *The Army Air Forces in World War II:*
Vol. 4, *The Pacific: Guadalcanal to Saipan, August 1942 to July 1944.* University of Chicago Press, 1950.
Vol. 5, *The Pacific: Matterhorn to Nagasaki, June 1944 to August 1945.* University of Chicago Press, 1953.

Cries for Peace: Experiences of Japanese Victims of World War II. Compiled by the Youth Division of Soka Gakkai. Tokyo: The Japan Times, 1978.

Crighton, R. A., *Japanese Popular Prints: 1700-1900.* Victoria and Albert Museum, Her Majesty's Stationery Office, 1973.

de Bary, Wm. Theodore, ed., *Sources of the Japanese Tradition.* Compiled by Ryusaku Tsunoda, Wm. Theodore de Bary and Donald Keene. Columbia University Press, 1958.

Dore, Ronald P., *Shinohata: A Portrait of a Japanese Village.* Pantheon Books, 1978.

Editors of Fortune, The, *Japan.* Overseas Editions, 1944.

Emmerson, John K., *The Japanese Thread: A Life in the U.S. Foreign Service.* Holt, Rinehart and Winston, 1978.

Feis, Herbert, *The Road to Pearl Harbor.* Atheneum, 1965.

Foreign Affairs Association of Japan, The:
The Japan Year Book, 1941-42. The Japan Times Press.
The Japan Year Book, 1943-44. The Japan Times Press.

Gibney, Frank, *Five Gentlemen of Japan.* Farrar, Straus and Young, 1953.

Glines, Carroll V., *Doolittle's Tokyo Raiders.* D. Van Nostrand, 1964.

Goette, John, *Japan Fights for Asia.* Harcourt, Brace, 1943.

Goldberg, Alfred, ed., *A History of the United States Air Force.* D. Van Nostrand, 1974.

Grew, Joseph C.:
Ten Years in Japan. Simon and Schuster, 1944.
Turbulent Era: A Diplomatic Record of Forty Years, 1904-1945. Houghton Mifflin, 1952.

Guillain, Robert, *Le Peuple Japonais et la Guerre: Choses Vues, 1939-1946.* Paris: René Julliard, 1946.

Hadley, Eleanor M., *Antitrust in Japan.* Princeton University Press, 1970.

Halloran, Richard, *Japan: Images and Realities.* Alfred A. Knopf, 1969.

Havens, Thomas R. H., *Valley of Darkness.* W. W. Norton, 1978.

Hayashi, Saburo, with Alvin D. Coox, *Kogun: The Japanese Army in the Pacific War.* Greenwood Press, 1959.

Hewes, Laurence I., Jr., *Japan—Land and Men: An Account of the Japanese Land Reform Program—1945-1951.* Greenwood Press, 1955.

Ichiokunin no Showa Shi:
Vol. 1, *Koritsu e no Michi.* Tokyo: Mainichi Shimbunsha, 1975.
Vol. 2, *2/26 Jiken to Nitchu Senso.* Tokyo: Mainichi Shimbunsha, 1975.
Vol. 3, *Taiheiyo Senso.* Tokyo: Mainichi Shimbunsha, 1975.
Vol. 4, *Kushu, Haisen, Hikiage.* Tokyo: Mainichi Shimbunsha, 1975.

Ienaga, Saburo, *The Pacific War: World War II and the Japanese, 1931-1945.* Pantheon Books, 1968.

Ike, Nobutaka, ed. and transl., *Japan's Decision for War: Records of the 1941 Policy Conference.* Stanford University Press, 1967.

Ikeda, Norizane, *Hinomaru Hour.* Tokyo: Chuokoronsha, 1979.

Inoguchi, Rikihei, and Tadashi Nakajima, with Roger Pineau, *The Divine Wind.* United States Naval Institute, 1958.

Iriye, Akira, *Across the Pacific: An Inner History of American-East Asian Relations.* Harcourt, Brace & World, 1967.

Iwasaki, Akira, *Nihon Eiga Shi.* Tokyo: Asahi Shimbunsha, 1977.

Jablonski, Edward, *Airwar,* Vols. 3 and 4. Doubleday, 1971.

Johnson, Sheila K., *American Attitudes toward Japan, 1941-1975.* American Enterprise Institute for Public Policy Research, 1975.

Jones, F. C., *Japan's New Order in East Asia: Its Rise and Fall, 1937-45.* Oxford University Press, 1954.

Kageyama, Koyo:
Shashin Showa 50-nen Shi. Tokyo: Kodansha International, 1975.
Showa no Onna. Tokyo: Asahi Shimbunsha, 1965.

Kase, Toshikazu, *Journey to the "Missouri."* Ed. by David Nelson Rowe. Archon Books, 1950.

Kato, Masuo, *The Lost War: A Japanese Reporter's Inside Story.* Alfred A. Knopf, 1946.

Kodama, Yoshio, *I Was Defeated.* Japan: Robert Booth and Taro Fukuda, 1951.

Lane, Richard, *Masters of the Japanese Print: Their World and Their Work.* Doubleday, 1962.

Latourette, Kenneth Scott, *A Short History of the Far East.* Macmillan, 1946.

Livingston, Jon, Joe Moore and Felicia Oldfather, eds., *Imperial Japan: 1800-1945.* Pantheon Books, 1973.

Lory, Hillis, *Japan's Military Masters: The Army in Japanese Life.* Viking, 1943.

Maraini, Fosco, *Meeting with Japan.* Transl. by Eric Mosbacher. Viking, 1959.

Maraini, Fosco, and the Editors of Time-Life Books, *Tokyo* (The Great Cities series). Amsterdam: Time-Life Books, 1976.

Maruyama, Masao, *Thought and Behavior in Modern Japanese Politics.* Ed. by Ivan Morris. London: Oxford University Press, 1963.

Matsuoka, Yoko, *Daughter of the Pacific.* Greenwood Press, 1952.

Me de miru Showa. Tokyo: Asahi Shimbunsha, 1972.

Meiji 100-nen no Rekishi, Vol. 3. Tokyo: Kodansha International, 1960.

Mikesh, Robert C., *Smithsonian Annals of Flight, No. 9, Japan's World War II Balloon Bomb Attacks on North America.* Smithsonian Institution Press, 1973.

Millot, Bernard, *Divine Thunder: The Life and Death of the Kamikazes.* Transl. by Lowell Bair. McCall Publishing, 1971.

Minear, Richard H., *Victors' Justice: The Tokyo War Crimes Trial.* Princeton University Press, 1971.

Morison, Samuel Eliot, "Old Bruin": Commodore Matthew C. Perry, 1794-1858.* Little, Brown, 1967.

Morris, Ivan, *The Nobility of Failure: Tragic Heroes in the History of Japan.* New American Library, 1975.

Mosley, Leonard, *Hirohito: Emperor of Japan.* Prentice-Hall, 1966.

Musashi, Miyamoto, *A Book of Five Rings.* Transl. by Victor Harris. The Overlook Press, 1974.

Nakamoto, Hiroko, as told to Mildred Mastin Pace, *My Japan: 1930-1951.* McGraw-Hill, 1970.

Nihon Hyakunen no Kiroku, Vol. 3. Tokyo: Kodansha International, 1961.

Nihon Kushu. Tokyo: Mainichi Shimbunsha, 1971.

Nihon no Rekishi, Vol. 19, *Taisho/Showa no Shuyaku.* Tokyo: Akatsuki Kyoiku Tosho, 1976.

Nihon Senbotsu Gakusei Shuki Henshu Iinkai, ed., *Kike Wadatsumi no Koe.* University of Tokyo Press, 1952.

The Nippon Times. Tokyo: 1943-1945.

Okada, Sadahiro, *Okada Keisuke Taiko-roku.* Tokyo: Mainichi Shimbunsha, 1977.

Olson, Lawrence, *Dimensions of Japan.* American Universities Field Staff, 1963.

Pacific War Research Society, The:
The Day Man Lost: Hiroshima, 6 August 1945. Kodansha International, 1972.
Japan's Longest Day. Kodansha International, 1968.

Potter, John Deane, *Yamamoto: The Man Who Menaced America.* Viking, 1965.

Reischauer, Edwin O.:
Japan: Past and Present. Alfred A. Knopf, 1964.
Japan: The Story of a Nation. Alfred A. Knopf, 1970.
The Japanese. Harvard University Press, 1977.

Rice, Richard, "Economic Mobilization in Wartime Japan: Business, Bureaucracy and Military in Conflict." *Journal of Asian Studies,* Vol. 38, No. 4, August 1979.

Roberts, John G., *Mitsui: Three Centuries of Japanese Business.* John Weatherhill, 1973.

Robinson, B. W., *The Arts of the Japanese Sword.* London: Faber and Faber, 1961.

Sakai, Atsuharu, *Japan in a Nutshell: Religion, Culture, Popular Practices.* Yokohama: Yamagata Printing, 1949.

Sakai, Saburo, with Martin Caidin and Fred Saito. *Samurai!* Bantam Books, 1957.

Sakamaki, Kazuo, *I Attacked Pearl Harbor.* Transl. by Toru Matsumoto. Association Press, 1949.

Sansom, G. B., *Japan: A Short Cultural History.* D. Appleton-Century, 1943.

Sekaishi no Naka no Ichiokunin no Showa Shi:
Vol. 2, *Sekai Kokyo kara Manshu Jiken e 1926-1932.* Tokyo: Mainichi Shimbunsha, 1978.
Vol. 3, *2/26 Jiken to Daisan Teikoku.* Tokyo: Mainichi Shimbunsha, 1978.

Shigemitsu, Mamoru, *Japan and Her Destiny: My Struggle for Peace.* Ed. by F. S. G. Piggott and transl. by Oswald White. E. P. Dutton, 1958.

Shigenori, Togo, *The Cause of Japan.* Ed. and transl. by Togo Fumihiko and Ben Bruce Blakeney. Greenwood Press, 1956.

Shiroyama, Saburo, *War Criminal: The Life and Death of Hirota Koki.* Transl. by John Bester. Kodansha International, 1977.

Showa Nihon Shi:
Vol. 2, *Gunka no Hibiki.* Tokyo: Akatsuki Kyoiku Tosho, 1977.
Vol. 3, *Nitchu Senso.* Tokyo: Akatsuki Kyoiku Tosho, 1977.
Vol. 4, *Taiheiyo Senso/Zenki.* Tokyo: Akatsuki Kyoiku Tosho, 1977.
Vol. 5, *Taiheiyo Senso/Koki.* Tokyo: Akatsuki Kyoiku Tosho, 1977.

Vol. 7, *Senso to Minshu*. Tokyo: Akatsuki Kyoiku Tosho, 1977.

Vol. 8, *Shusen no Hiroku*. Tokyo: Akatsuki Kyoiku Tosho, 1976.

Bekkan (Special edition), *Koshitsu no Hanseiki*. Tokyo: Akatsuki Kyoiku Tosho, 1977.

Smith, Bradley, *Japan—A History in Art*. Gemini, 1964.

Staff of *Ashai Shimbun*, The, *The Pacific Rivals: A Japanese View of Japanese-American Relations*. Transl. by Ken'ichi Otsuka, Peter Grilli and Yoshio Murakami. John Weatherhill, 1972.

Staff of the *Mainichi Daily News*, The, *Fifty Years of Light and Dark: The Hirohito Era*. Tokyo: The Mainichi Newspapers, 1975.

Storry, Richard:

The Double Patriots: A Study of Japanese Nationalism. London: Chatto and Windus, 1957.

A History of Modern Japan. Penguin Books, 1960.

The Way of the Samurai. G. P. Putnam's Sons, 1978.

Tanizaki, Junichiro, *The Makioka Sisters*. Transl. by Edward Seidensticker. Charles E. Tuttle, 1958.

Terasaki, Gwen, *Bridge to the Sun*. University of North Carolina Press, 1957.

Thompson, Paul W., Harold Doud, John Scofield, and Milton A. Hill, *How the Jap Army Fights*. Infantry Journal and Penguin Books, 1942.

Tillitse, Lars, "When Bombs Rained on Us in Tokyo." *Saturday Evening Post*, January 12, 1946.

Toland, John, *The Rising Sun: The Decline and Fall of the Japanese Empire, 1936-1945*. Random House, 1970.

Tsuneishi, Warren M., *Japanese Political Style*. Harper & Row, 1966.

Turnbull, S. R., *The Samurai: A Military History*. Macmillan, 1977.

Uhlan, Edward, and Dana L. Thomas, *Shoriki: Miracle Man of Japan*. Exposition Press, 1957.

The United States Strategic Bombing Survey:

The Effects of Bombing on Health and Medical Services in Japan, October 24-November 31, 1945. Medical Division, June 1947.

The Effects of Strategic Bombing on Japanese Morale. Morale Division, June 1947.

Wilson, George Macklin, "Kita Ikki, Okawa Shumei and the Yuzonsha: A Study in the Genesis of Showa Nationalism," *Papers on Japan*, Vol. 2. East Asian Research Center, Harvard University, August 1943.

PICTURE CREDITS

Credits from left to right are separated by semicolons, from top to bottom by dashes.

COVER and page 1: *Mainichi Shimbun*, Tokyo. 2, 3: Map by Tarijy Elsab.

THE ROAD TO PEARL HARBOR—8-12: *Mainichi Shimbun*, Tokyo. 13: National Archives (No. 306-NT-1151E-13). 14, 15: *Asahi Shimbun*, Tokyo; National Archives (No. 306-NT-1154K-11). 16, 17: *Mainichi Shimbun*, Tokyo. 18: UPI. 19: UPI; Cable News Agency, Tokyo; insets: Kyodo News, Tokyo; *Asahi Shimbun*, Tokyo (2)—Wide World. 20, 21: *Asahi Shimbun*, Tokyo—*Mainichi Shimbun*, Tokyo; *Asahi Shimbun*, Tokyo; *Mainichi Shimbun*, Tokyo. 22, 23: Kyodo News, Tokyo—Shinji Sato, Tokyo; *Asahi Shimbun*, Tokyo (4). 24: *Mainichi Shimbun*, Tokyo—*Asahi Shimbun*, Tokyo. 25: *Asahi Shimbun*, Tokyo. 26, 27: UPI.

THE SPIRIT OF JAPAN—30: Kyodo News, Tokyo—*Asahi Shimbun*, Tokyo. 33: Tadao Umemoto, Tokyo. 36: Kabukiza, Tokyo. 38: *Mainichi Shimbun*, Tokyo. 40: The Bettmann Archive.

PREPARING FOR THE BOMBERS—42, 43: Wide World. 44: *Mainichi Shimbun*, Tokyo. 45: Natori from Black Star. 46, 47: *Mainichi Shimbun*, Tokyo (2). 48, 49: Wide World; UPI—*Berliner Illustrierte Zeitung*, Berlin. 50, 51: Tadao Umemoto, Tokyo—*Asahi Shimbun*, Tokyo; *Mainichi Shimbun*, Tokyo. 52, 53: UPI.

TOJO AND THE TOOLS OF WAR—56: *Mainichi Shimbun*, Tokyo. 60: Koyo Kageyama, Fujisawa-Shi. 63: Takeo Shinmyo, Tokyo.

THE GOSPEL OF PATRIOTISM—66, 67: Kodansha, Tokyo. 68: Buko Shimizu, Chichibu-Shi. 69: *Asahi Shimbun*, Tokyo. 70, 71: *Mainichi Shimbun*, Tokyo; Koyo Kageyama, Fujisawa-Shi; bottom right Kodansha, Tokyo. 72, 73: Buko Shimizu, Chichibu-Shi, except top left, Koyo Kageyama, Fujisawa-Shi. 74: Top, UPI. 75: Wide World. 76, 77: Tadao Umemoto, Tokyo.

THE IMPERIAL CAPTIVE—80, 81: Central Press Photos Ltd., London. 82, 83: Imperial Household Agency, Tokyo. 84: BBC Hulton Picture Library, London; Wide World—Imperial Household Agency, Tokyo (2). 85: Imperial Household Agency, Tokyo. 86: *Mainichi Shimbun*, Tokyo, except bottom left, Koyo Kageyama, Fujisawa-Shi. 87: Kyodo News, Tokyo. 88: Imperial Household Agency, Tokyo—UPI. 89: Jiji Tsushin, Tokyo. 90, 91: Wide World; *Asahi Shimbun*, Tokyo.

IN THE VALLEY OF DARKNESS—94: Akatsuki Kyoiku Tosho, Tokyo. 96: *Asahi Shimbun*, Tokyo. 97-99: UPI.

TOO LITTLE OF EVERYTHING—102, 103: Koyo Kageyama, Fujisawa-Shi. 104,

105: *Mainichi Shimbun*, Tokyo. 106: Buko Shimizu, Chichibu-Shi—Koyo Kageyama, Fujisawa-Shi. 107: Buko Shimizu, Chichibu-Shi. 108: Buko Shimizu, Chichibu-Shi; Motoichi Kumagai, Kiyose-Shi—courtesy Carl Mydans; Koyo Kageyama, Fujisawa-Shi. 109: Koyo Kageyama, Fujisawa-Shi; *Mainichi Shimbun*, Tokyo—Wide World; Jyo Kondo, Yonago-Shi. 110, 111: *Mainichi Shimbun*, Tokyo.

WOMEN'S WORK—112, 113: *Mainichi Shimbun*, Tokyo. 114: Keystone. 115: Koyo Kageyama, Fujisawa-Shi. 116, 117: UPI; Koyo Kageyama, Fujisawa-Shi. 118, 119: *Mainichi Shimbun*, Tokyo; Buko Shimizu, Chichibu-Shi. 120, 121: *Asahi Shimbun*, Tokyo; Tadao Umemoto, Tokyo.

THE MILITARY LIFE—125: *Asahi Shimbun*, Tokyo. 126, 128: *Yomiuri Shimbun*, Tokyo. 129, 130: *Mainichi Shimbun*, Tokyo.

A NATION OF SAMURAI—132, 133: Derek Bayes, courtesy Victoria and Albert Museum, London. 134: UPI. 135: E. G. Heath Collection, Whitstable, England. 136: Victoria and Albert Museum, Crown Copyright, London—Werner Forman Archive, courtesy Victoria and Albert Museum, London (2). 137: *Mainichi Shimbun*, Tokyo. 138, 139: Seiji Nagata, photographed by Masachika Suhara, Tokyo—Wide World. 140, 141: © Bradley Smith—Shunkichi Kikuchi, Tokyo.

A COUNTRY TOWN AT WAR—142-153: Buko Shimizu, Chichibu-Shi.

A SPRINGTIME OF FIRE—156: Shunkichi Kikuchi, Tokyo. 158: UPI—Koyo Kageyama, Fujisawa-Shi. 159: *Asahi Shimbun*, Tokyo—Koyo Kageyama, Fujisawa-Shi. 160-165: *Mainichi Shimbun*, Tokyo. 167: *Asahi Shimbun*, Tokyo.

DESTRUCTION FROM THE SKY—170, 171: *Mainichi Shimbun*, Tokyo. 172: Koyo Kageyama, Fujisawa-Shi. 173-179: *Mainichi Shimbun*, Tokyo. 180, 181: Koyo Ishikawa, Tokyo.

LOST BATTLES, LAST HOPES—184: *Mainichi Shimbun*, Tokyo. 185: Kiyoshi Tanaka, courtesy Bert Webber from *Retaliation: Japanese Attacks and Allied Countermeasures on the Pacific Coast in World War II*, Oregon State University Press, 1975. 186, 187: *Mainichi Shimbun*, Tokyo. 188: Shunkichi Kikuchi, Tokyo. 191, 192: *Asahi Shimbun*, Tokyo.

DAYS OF DESPERATION—194, 195: *Mainichi Shimbun*, Tokyo. 196, 197: Shunkichi Kikuchi, Tokyo. 198, 199: Shigeo Hayashi, Tokyo; Kodansha, Tokyo. 200, 201: *Mainichi Shimbun*, Tokyo. 202, 203: U.S. Air Force; *Mainichi Shimbun*, Tokyo.

ACKNOWLEDGMENTS

For help given in the preparation of this book, the editors wish to express their gratitude to Hans Becker, ADN-Zentralbild, Berlin, DDR; Yayoi Cooke, East Asia Library, University of Maryland, College Park; Aksuko Craft, East Asia Library, University of Maryland, College Park; Connie Galmeijer, East Asia Library, University of Maryland, College Park; Merle Goldman, Associate Professor of History, Boston University, Boston; Minoru Hanazawa, *Asahi Shimbun*, Tokyo; Yuko Harada, Shimamoto, Japan; W. M. Hawley, Hollywood, California; Shigeo Hayashi, Tokyo; Shojo Honda, Senior Reference Librarian, Japanese Section, Library of Congress, Washington, D.C.; The Imperial Household Agency, Tokyo; Koyo Kageyama, Fujisawa, Japan; Yoshio Kawashima, *Mainichi Shimbun*, Tokyo; Shunkichi Kikuchi, Tokyo; Key Kobayashi, Japanese Section, Library of Congress, Washington, D.C.; Jyo Kondo, Yonago, Japan; Colonel Nikio Kuga, Embassy of Japan, Defense Section, Washington, D.C.; Robert C. Mikesh, National Air and Space Museum, The Smithsonian Institution, Washington, D.C.; Koji Morooka, Tokyo; Philip Nagao, Japanese Section, Library of Congress, Washington, D.C.; D. B. Nash, Imperial War Museum, London; Erik Neumann, U.S. National Arboretum, Washington, D.C.; Fumi Norcia, Japanese Section, Library of Congress, Washington, D.C.; Yasuyori Okuda, Alexandria, Virginia; George Phebus, Natural History Museum, The Smithsonian Institution, Washington, D.C.; Shirley Quainbush, East Asia Library, University of Maryland, College Park; B. W. Robinson, London; Axel Schulz, Ullstein Bilderdienst, Berlin (West); Abbot Eido Shimano, *Daibosatsu Zendo*, Livingston Manor, New York; Buko Shimizu, Chichibu, Japan; J. S. Simmonds, Imperial War Museum, London; Bradley Smith, Gemini Smith, Inc., La Jolla, California; Marilyn Murphy Terrell, Alexandria, Virginia; Dr. Nathaniel B. Thayer, School of Advanced International Studies, Johns Hopkins University, Washington, D.C.; Dr. Haruo Tsuchiya, Yamagata City, Japan; Bunzo Tsujiguchi, *Mainichi Shimbun*, Tokyo; Chieko Ui, Tokyo; Alan Weatherley, Alexandria, Virginia; Jennifer Wood, Imperial War Museum, London; The Reverend Mr. Susumu Yoshida, Honolulu.

The index for this book was prepared by Nicholas J. Anthony.

205

INDEX

Numerals in italics indicate an illustration of the subject mentioned.

A

Aikawa, Takaaki, 124, 131
Air raids: American sorties, 44, *50-51*, *90-91*, 154-157, 160, *164-165*, 166-169, *170-181*, *194-203*; bomb tonnages expended, 169; carrier-based, 44, 155, 166, 168-169, 172; children in civil defense, *50*, 51; civilian reaction to, 162, 169; damage assessments, 169; defensive measures against, *42-53*, 57, 154-155, *156*, 157, 160-161, 183; effect of winds on, 161, 168, 172; students in civil defense, *50*; women in civil defense, 44, *45-47*, *49*. *See also by locality*
Aircraft carriers, sorties from, 44, 155, 166, 168-169, 172
Aircraft production: American, 126, 155; Japanese, 62-65, 95-96, *112-113*, *115*, *120*, 161, 169, 188
Aircraft strength, claims of, 184
Airfields, strikes against, 168-169
Akazawa, Tomie, 168-169
Akihito, Crown Prince of Japan, *84*
Akutagawa, Ryunosuke, 129
Amagasaki, air raid on, *200-201*
Amaterasu (sun goddess), 29-31
Araki, Sadao, 16, 18, 20
Armed forces: command and control, policy of, 65; life in, 122-131; strength of, estimated, 124, 184; women in, *140*
Asahi (newspaper), *20-21*
Asahi, Heigo, 14
Asakusa Temple, 42-43
Asano, Lord, 139
Assassinations, *18-19*, *22-23*, *86*, 87
Atrocities, by Army: 61-62, 98
Attu Island, occupation of, 65
Austerity program, 70, *94*, 96

B

Baseball, in wartime, 101, *128*
Bathhouses, fuel for, 95
Benkai (priest), *132*
Black market, 93-94, 97, 100, 104, 185
Blood Brotherhood, *18*, *19*
Bomb types: balloon bombs, *185*; demolition, 156, 160, 166; incendiary, 154-155, 157, 160-161, 164, 166-169, *170-171*, 172, *174-175*, *176-177*, 179-181, *187*, 196-197, *202-203*; napalm, 161, 174
Bonin Islands, 161
Borneo, 64
Boyle, Martin, 164, 166-167
Buddhism, 32
Burma, 60-62
Bushido (Way of the Warrior), 40-41, 127-131, 187-188

C

Cabinet: Information Bureau, 122; Planning Board, 62, 65; powers of, 55; unification sought, 157
Camouflage, use of, *52-53*, *134*, 156
Caroline Islands, 41, 65
Casualties: in China campaigns, 29, 78; Chinese, 98; civilian, 3, 29, 154-155, 160-164, 166-169, 172, *180-181*; Japanese Army, 29, 78; Korean, 98
Celebes, 65
Censorship, *20-21*, 24, 57-59, 100-101
Chamberlain, Neville, 55
Chichibu, *142-153*

Children: in civil defense, *50*, 51; evacuation and relocation of, *158-159*; in labor force, 73, 98-99, *116*, *146-147*, 185, *187*; military indoctrination of, *38*, 57, *74*, 123-124, 134, 186-187
China: American air bases in, 156; attempted invasions of, 33; casualties in, 29, 78; cultural and trade relations with, 31, 34; in Greater East Asia Co-Prosperity Sphere, 60; war with, 24, 29, 41, 60
Chinese: atrocities against, 61, 98; casualties among, 98; in labor force, 97-98
Christianity, introduction of, 32, 34
Chuken shoko, 55-56
Civil defense. *See* Air raids
Civilians: casualties among, 3, 29, 154-155, 160-164, 166-169, 172, *180-181*; evacuation and relocation of, 51, 156, *158-159*, 163, *167*, 168-169, *194-195*, *196*, *198*; in homeland defense, 183-186; suicides among, 98, 140, 196
Clothing, shortages of, *70*, 92, 101
Colonialism, ventures in, 10, *16-17*, 26, 33-34, 41
Communists: abhorrence of, 15, 190; rallies by, *14-15*
Conscription: 124-125, 128, 155, 183; adopted, 39; Army control of, 64-65, 95-96; for homeland defense, 183; physical standards for, *129*; of students, *130*; of veterans, 183; of women, 114
Cost of living, rises in, 97
Cotton imports, decline of, 92-93
Crime, control and spread of, 57, 185
Cultural activities, curtailment of, 100

D

Dan, Takuma, 18, *19*
Dead, veneration of, *78-79*, 130-131, *145*, *152-153*
Death, attitude toward, 36, 131, 134, 139-140, 187-189. *See also* Suicide
Defeatists, arrests of, 184
Defense industries. *See* War industries
Deguchi, Wanisaburo, *21*
Diet (Parliament): Army conflict with, 20, *25*, 54-56; powers of, 37; Tojo in, *56*
Dissidence. *See* Subversive activities
Doolittle Raid, 44, 155, 172
Draft. *See* Conscription
Dutch East Indies, 41, 62, 64

E

Earthquakes, destruction from, 10, 155
Economic police, 94, 100
Economy, deterioration of, 10, 13-14, 29, 92-97, 104, 144
Educational system, 36-37, 55, 123-124
Emperor of Japan: divinity, myth of, 30-31, 37; restoration of, 37, 39, 62; veneration of, 10, 21, 38-39, 58, 123, 125, 131, 186, 189. *See also* Hirohito, Emperor of Japan
Entertainment and recreation, 34, *60*, 100-101. *See also* Sports
Etajima, 131

F

Farmers: associations of, 57; contributions by, *146-149*; in Depression, *12*, 13; discontent among, 14-15, 99-100, 144; in homeland defense, 183, 185-186; production by, *12*, 13, 30, 71, 93-94, 98-100, *107*, 146-149, 159, 183-185, 198
Financial panic, *11*, 13
Firearms, introduction of, 33
Fishing, control of, 101
Food production and shortages, *12*, 13, 30, 71, 93-94, 98-100, *104-107*, 146-149,

159, 183-185, 198
Formosa. *See* Taiwan
Forty-seven *ronin*, *138-139*
Francis Xavier, 32
Fuel shortages, 95-96, *98-99*, *102-103*, 104, 109-110, 183, *187*
Fuji, Mount, *71*, 129
Fujihara, Ginjiro, 62-63, 65
Fujiwara, Kamatari, 31-32
Fushimi, Prince, 157

G

Gas-mask drill, *42-43*, *46-47*
Geisha, 34, *144*, 146, *149*
George V, King of Great Britain, *84*
Germany, treaty with, 26
Gifu, air raid on, 168
Gilbert Islands campaign, 156
Gomikawa, Junpei, 28-29
Great Britain. *See* United Kingdom
Greater East Asia Co-Prosperity Sphere, 60-62
Guadalcanal campaign, 183
Guerrilla warfare, 62, 184, 187
Guillain, Robert, 28, 164
Gyokusai, 183, 189

H

Hair styles, regulation of, 70, 96
Hall of the Baying Deer, 36-37
Hamada, Kunimatsu, *24*
Hamaguchi, Osachi, *18*
Hangan, Lord, 36
Hara-kiri. *See* Suicide
Hasegawa, Kiyoshi, 190
Hasegawa, Shin, 130
Hibiya Park, 101, 125
Hirohito, Emperor of Japan: ancestry, 31; on Army-Navy cooperation, 62, 65; assassination attempts on, *86*, 87; aversion to war, 28, 88, 90, 189; in ceremonial robes, *85*; decision process, role in, 56, 88; and divinity principle, 82, 87-88; education and rearing, 82-83; enthronement, 31, *85*; European tour, *80-81*, *84*, 87; family life, *84*; and homeland defense plans, 191; imperial rescripts by, 28-29, 59; inspects air-raid damage, *90-91*, 160, 164, 168, 191; isolation of, *90*; and Leyte campaign, 182; and militarists, 82, 87-88; morale-boosting by, 59, 183; and mutiny of 1936, 23; and peace negotiations, 189-193; powers of, 55, 86-88; scientific pursuits, 82; status of, preserving, 87, 186, 189-190; Tojo, relations with, 157; and veneration of dead, 78; veneration by subjects, *86-87*, 89, 123, 125, 131; and war capability, 29; and War Council, *88*; Western customs, influence on, *84*; at Yamamoto funeral, 122. *See also* Emperor of Japan
Hiroshima, *109*, 196
Hitachi electrical company, 95
Hitler, Adolf, 26, 55
Homeland, defense of, *140-141*, 183-187, *191*, 196; conscription for, 183; farmers in, 183, 185-186; fortifications for, 187, *191*; plans for repelling invasion, 140, 183-187, *191*, 196; students in, 183, 186-187; women in, 183-185; youths in, 183, 185
Hornet, U.S.S., 155
Hoshino, Naoki, 61
Hyuga, 64

I

Ichigaya, 183
Iida, Minoru, 154
Ikeda, Norizane, 101
Imperial Palace, *160*, 167-168
Imperial rescripts: on declaration of war, 28-

Printed in U.S.A.